CW00573593

PHRASE BOOK

COLLINS
London and Glasgow

First published 1986

Consultant
Marisa Rusconi

ISBN 0 00 459403-7

Other Travel Gem
Phrase Books:

French

German

Spanish

Your **Travel Gem** Phrase Book will prove an invaluable companion on your holiday or trip abroad. In a genuinely handy format, it gives you all you need to say for basic communication, with fast and direct alphabetical access to the relevant information. Be sure to pack it with your passport!

Its layout provides two means of quick alphabetical access:

99 practical topics arranged in A-to-Z order from ACCOMMODATION to WINTER SPORTS via such topics as MENUS, ROOM SERVICE and TAXIS. Each topic gives you the basic phrases you will need, and in many cases an additional list with useful extra words. Just flick through the pages to the topic you need to look up;

an alphabetical index at the back - WORDS - listing up to 1400 key words found in the 99 topics, for fast access to words which do not immediately seem to belong to a particular topic (such as 'safety pin, lose, passport').

This way you have the possibility of browsing through topics, as in more traditional phrase books, as well as having the advantage of alphabetical listing. The best of both worlds.

For information on GRAMMAR, PRONUNCIATION, the ALPHABET or CONVERSION CHARTS, , just flick through the pages until you get to that topic in alphabetical order. Though **Travel Gems** do not assume prior knowledge of the foreign language, some basic facts about grammar will help you improvise and get more out of your conversations with local people.

Whenever relevant, travel information has been included. Some likely replies to what you might say have also been shown in several topics (such as DENTIST or DOCTOR).

Enjoy your stay!

For a traffic offence, Italian police have the power to fine you on the spot.

There's been an accident C'è stato un incidente
che stahto oon eenchee-dentay

I've crashed my car Ho distrutto la macchina
o deestroot-to la mak-keena

Can I see your insurance certificate please? Posso vedere la sua assicurazione per favore?
pos-so vay-dayray la soo-a as-seekoo-rats-yohnay payr fa-vohray

We will have to report it to the police Dovremo comunicarlo alla polizia
do-vraymo komoo-neekahr-lo al-la poleet-see-a

Call the police! Chiamate la polizia!
kee-a-mahtay la poleet-see-a

He ran into me Mi è venuto contro
mee e vay-nooto kohntro

I ran into him Gli sono andato contro
lyee sohnoh an-dahto kohntroh

He was driving too fast Guidava troppo forte
gwee-dahva trop-po fortay

He was too close Era troppo vicino
ayra trop-po vee-cheeno

He did not give way Non ha dato la precedenza
nohn a dahto la praychay-dentsa

The car number was ... La targa era ...
la tahrga ayra ...

He was coming from my right/left Veniva dalla mia destra/sinistra
vay-neeva dal-la mee-a destra/see-neestra

damage
il danno
dan-no

documents
i documenti
dokoo-mayntee

driving licence
la patente
pa-tentay

green card
la carta verde
kahrta vayrday

insurance company
la compagnia di assicurazione
kompan-yee-a dee as-seekoo-rats-yohnay

law
la legge
layd-jay

lawyer
un avvocato
av-vo-kahto

offence
la contravvenzione
kontrav-vaynts-yohnay

police station
il posto di polizia
pohstoh dee poleet-see-a

See also EMERGENCIES.
Dial 113 for ambulance, fire, police. Ambulances have to be paid for.

There has been an accident C'è stato un incidente
che stahto oon eenchee-dentay

Call an ambulance/a doctor Chiamate un'ambulanza/un dottore
kee-a-mahtay oonam-boolant-sa/oon doht-tohray

He has hurt himself Si è fatto male
see e faht-to mahlay

I am hurt Mi sono fatto male
mee sohnoh faht-to mahlay

He is seriously injured/bleeding È ferito gravemente/Perde sangue
e fay-reeto grahvay-mayntay/payrday sangwe

He can't breathe/move Non può respirare/muoversi
nohn pwo rayspee-rahray/mwo-vayrsee

I can't move my arm/leg Non posso muovere il braccio/la gamba
nohn pos-so mwo-vayray eel brat-cho/la gamba

Cover him up Copritelo
kopree-telo

Don't move him Non muovetelo
nohn mwovay-telo

He has broken his arm/cut himself Ha rotto il braccio/Si è tagliato
a rot-to eel brat-cho/see e tal-yahto

I have had a fall Sono caduto
sohnoh ka-dooto

bandage
la benda
benda

bite, to
mordere
mor-dayray

dead
morto
morto

dislocate, to
slogare
zlo-gahray

hospital
un ospedale
ospay-dahlay

serious
grave
grahvay

slip, to
scivolare
sheevo-lahray

sprain
la storta
storta

stung
punto
poonto

sunburn
la scottatura solare
skot-ta-toora so-lahray

sunstroke
un'insolazione
eenso-lats-yohnay

See also HOTEL DESK, ROOM SERVICE, SELF-CATERING.

Hotels are officially graded from one to five stars, while boarding houses (*pensioni*) are also grouped into three categories. Prices are usually per room, and you will have to pay an extra 17% service charge and IVA (VAT).

I want to reserve a single/double room
Vorrei prenotare una camera singola/matrimoniale
vor-re-ee prayno-tahray oona ka-mayra seen-gohla/matree-mohn-yahlay

Is there a restaurant/bar? C'è un ristorante/bar?
che oon reesto-rantay/bar

I want bed and breakfast/full board
Vorrei una camera con prima colazione/pensione completa
vor-re-ee oona ka-mayra kohn preema kolats-yohnay/pensee-ohnay komple-ta

What is the daily/weekly rate?
Quanto costa al giorno/alla settimana?
kwanto kohsta al jorno/al-la sayt-tee-mahna

Is breakfast included in the price? La colazione è compresa nel prezzo?
la kolats-yohnay e kom-prayza nel prets-so

I want to stay three nights/from ... till ... Voglio restare per tre notti/dal ... fino al ...
vol-yo rays-tahray payr tray not-tee/dal ... feeno al ...

We'll be arriving at 7 p.m. Arriveremo alle 19.00
ar-reevay-raymo al-lay deechan-novay

Shall I confirm by letter? Devo mandare una conferma scritta?
dayvo man-dahray oona kon-fayrma skreet-ta

balcony
il balcone
bal-kohnay

bathroom
il bagno
ban-yo

double bed
letto matrimoniale
let-to matree-mon-yahlay

evening meal
la cena
chayna

half-board
la mezza pensione
medz-za payns-yohnay

lift
un ascensore
ashayn-sohray

single bed
letto a una piazza
let-to a oona pee-ats-sa

youth hostel
un ostello della gioventù
ostel-lo dayl-la jovayn-too

Where do I check in for the flight to Milan? Dov'è il check in del volo per Milano?
dohve eel check in del vohloh payr mee-lahno

Which departure gate do I go to? A quale uscita devo andare?
a kwahlay oo-sheeta dayvo an-dahray

I'd like an aisle/a window seat Vorrei un posto centrale/vicino al finestrino
vor-re-ee oon pohstoh chayn-trahlay/vee-cheeno al feenes-treeno

Will a meal be served on the plane? Daranno da mangiare sull'aereo?
daranno da man-jahray sool-la-e-ray-o

Where is the snack bar/duty-free shop? Dov'è il bar/duty free?
dohve eel bar/duty free

Where can I change some money? Dove posso cambiare i soldi?
dohvay pos-so kamb-yahray ee soldee

Where do I get the bus to town? Dove posso prendere l'autobus per la città?
dohvay pos-so pren-dayray low-toboos payr la cheet-ta

Where are the taxis/telephones? Dove sono i taxi/telefoni?
dohvay sohnoh ee taksee/tayle-fonee

I want to hire a car/reserve a hotel room Vorrei noleggiare una macchina/prenotare una stanza
vor-re-ee nolayd-jahray oona mak-keena/prayno-tahray oona stantsa

I am being met Mi stanno aspettando
mee stan-no aspayt-tando

---

airport
un aeroporto
a-ay-ropor-to

baggage reclaim
il ritiro bagagli
ree-teero bagal-yee

check-in desk
un'accettazione bagagli
at-chayt-tats-yohnay bagal-yee

flight
il volo
vohloh

lounge
la sala d'attesa
sahla dat-tayza

no smoking
vietato fumare
vee-ay-tahto foo-mahray

passport control
il controllo passaporti
kontrol-lo pas-sa-portee

plane
un aereo
a-e-ray-o

to land
atterrare
at-tayr-rahray

The Italian alphabet is the same as the English although native Italian words lack J, K, W, X and Y. The pronunciation of each letter is given below together with the word used conventionally for clarification when spelling something out.

A come	Ancona	N come	Napoli
a koh-*may*	*an-kohna*	*en-ne* koh-*may*	*nahpolee*
B for	Bari	O for	Otranto
bee	*bah-ree*	*o*	*o-tranto*
C	Catania	P	Palermo
chee	*katahnee-a*	*pee*	*palayr-mo*
D	Domodossola	Q	quarto
dee	*domo-dos-sola*	*koo*	*kwar-to*
E	Empoli	R	Roma
ay	*em-polee*	*er-re*	*roh-ma*
F	Firenze	S	Savona
ef-fe	*fee-rent-say*	*es-se*	*savoh-na*
G	Genova	T	Torino
jee	*jenohva*	*tee*	*toree-no*
H	Hotel	U	Udine
ak-ka	*oh-tel*	*oo*	*oodee-nay*
I	Imperia	V	Venezia
ee	*eem-payree-a*	*voo*	*vaynayt-see-a*
J		W	
ee loon-*goh*		*dop-pee-ohvoo*	
K		X	
kap-pa		*eex*	
L	Livorno	Y	
el-le	*lee-vorno*	*ee* gre-*koh*	
M	Milano	Z	
em-me	*mee-lahno*	*dze-ta*	

Is it far/expensive? È lontano/costa
molto?
*e lon-**tah**no/kohsta mohltoh*

Are you John Smith? Lei è John Smith?
le-ee e john smith

Do you understand? Ha capito?
*a ka-**peet**o*

Can I go in there? Posso entrare là dentro?
*pos-so ayn-**trah**ray la dayntro*

Can you help me? Può aiutarmi?
*pwo a-yoo-**tahr**mee*

Where are the shops? Dove sono i negozi?
*dohvay sohnoh ee nay-**gotse**e*

When will it be ready? Quando sarà pronto?
*kwando **sara** prohntoh*

How do I get there? Come faccio per andarci?
*kohmay fat-cho payr an-**dahr**chee*

How far/big is it? Quanto è distante/grande?
*kwanto e dee-**stan**tay/granday*

Is there a good restaurant? C'è un buon ristorante?
*che oon bwon reesto-**rant**ay*

What is this? Che cos'è questo?
*kay **koze** kwaysto*

Which is your room? Qual'è la sua stanza?
*kwa**hle** la soo-a stantsa*

Who is coming? Chi viene?
*kee vee-e-**nay***

How much is it? Quanto costa?
kwanto kohsta

How many kilometres? Quanti chilometri?
kwantee keelo-metree

Is this the bus for ...? E questo l'autobus per ...?
*e kwaysto **low**-toboos payr ...*

Changing rooms, as well as beach and sports items, can often be rented on the main beaches.

Is it safe to swim here? È pericoloso nuotare qui?
e payree-ko-lohzo nwo-tahray kwee

When is high/low tide? Quando c'è l'alta/la bassa marea?
kwando che lalta/la bas-sa ma-ray-a

How deep is the water? Quanto è profonda l'acqua?
kwanto e pro-fohnda lakwa

Are there strong currents? Ci sono correnti forti?
chee sohnoh kor-rentee fortee

Is it a private/quiet beach? È una spiaggia privata/tranquilla?
e oona spee-ad-ja pree-vahta/trankweel-la

Where do we change? Dove sono gli spogliatoi?
dohvay sohnoh lyee spol-yato-ee

Can I hire a deck chair? Posso prendere in affitto una sedia a sdraio?
pos-so pren-dayray een af-feet-to oona sed-ya a zdra-yo

Can I go fishing? Posso andare a pescare?
pos-so an-dahray a pay-skahray

Is there a children's pool? C'è una piscina per bambini?
che oona pee-sheena payr bam-beenee

Where can I get an ice-cream/ something to eat? Dove posso comprare un gelato/qualcosa da mangiare?
dohvay pos-so kom-prahray oon jay-lahto/kwal-koza da man-jahray

armbands	i bracciali *brat-chahlee*
bucket	il secchiello *sek-yayl-lo*
deck chair	la sedia a sdraio *sed-ya a zdra-yo*
lifeguard	il bagnino *ban-yeeno*
sea	il mare *mahray*
spade	la paletta *palayt-ta*
sunglasses	gli occhiali da sole *ok-yahlee da sohlay*
sunshade	un ombrellone *ombrayl-lohnay*
suntan oil	l'olio solare *ol-yo so-lahray*
swimsuit	il costume da bagno *ko-stoomay da ban-yo*
towel	un asciugamano *ashoo-ga-mahno*

ankle
la caviglia
kaveel-ya

arm
il braccio
brat-cho

back
la schiena
skee-e-na

body
il corpo
korpo

bone
un osso
os-so

breast
il petto
pet-to

buttocks
le natiche
nah-teekay

cheek
la guancia
gwancha

chest
il torace
to-rahchay

ear
un orecchio
orayk-yo

elbow
il gomito
goh-meetoh

eye
un occhio
ok-yo

face
la faccia
fat-cha

finger
il dito
deeto

foot
il piede
pee-e-day

hand
la mano
mahno

head
testa
testa

heart
il cuore
kworay

joint
un'articolazione
artee-kolats-yohnay

kidney
il rene
re-nay

knee
il ginocchio
jeenok-yo

leg
la gamba
gamba

liver
il fegato
fay-gato

lung
il polmone
pohl-mohnay

mouth
la bocca
bok-ka

muscle
il muscolo
moo-skolo

neck
il collo
kol-lo

nose
il naso
nahzo

shoulder
la spalla
spal-la

skin
la pelle
pel-lay

stomach
la pancia
pancha

throat
la gola
gohla

thumb
il pollice
pol-leechay

toe
il dito del piede
deeto dayl pee-e-day

tongue
la lingua
leengwa

wrist
il polso
pohlsoh

See also CAR PARTS.

Dial 116 for the ACI (*Automobile Club d'Italia*) which is affiliated to the AA and the RAC. Motorists must carry a triangular warning sign.

My car has broken down La mia
macchina si è rotta
la mee-a mak-keena see e roht-ta

**There is something wrong with the
brakes/electrics** C'è qualcosa che non va
nei freni/nell'impianto elettrico
*che kwal-koza kay nohn va nay-ee
fraynee/nel-leemp-yanto aylet-treeko*

I have run out of petrol Sono rimasto
senza benzina
sohnoh ree-masto sentsa bend-zeena

**There is a leak in the petrol
tank/radiator** Il serbatoio/radiatore
perde
eel sayrba-to-yo/rad-ya-tohray payrday

The windscreen has shattered Il
parabrezza si è rotto
eel para-braydz-za see e roht-to

The engine is overheating Il motore è
surriscaldato
eel moh-tohray e soor-reeskal-dahto

Can you tow me to a garage? Può
trainarmi da un meccanico?
*pwo tra-ee-nahrmee da oon mayk-ka-
neeko*

**Can you send a mechanic/a
breakdown van?** Può mandare un
meccanico/un carro attrezzi?
*pwo man-dahray oon mayk-ka-neeko/oon
kar-ro at-trets-see*

Do you have the parts? Avete i pezzi di
ricambio?
a-vaytay ee pets-see dee reekamb-yo

bulb
la lampadina
lampa-deena

flat tyre
la gomma a terra
gohm-ma a ter-ra

hazard lights
le luci d'emergenza
*loochay daymayr-
jayntsa*

jack
il cricco
kreek-ko

jump leads
i cavi per far
partire la macchina
*kahvee payr fahr
pahr-teeray la
mak-keena*

spanner
la chiave
kee-ahvay

tow rope
il cavo da
rimorchio
*kahvo da reemork-
yo*

warning triangle
il triangolo
tree-angolo

wheel brace
la chiave a tubo
kee-ahvay a toobo

I have an appointment with Signor Simone Ho un
appuntamento con il Signor Simone
*o oon ap-**poonta**-maynto kohn eel seen-**yor** see-**moh**nay*

He is expecting me Mi sta aspettando
*mee sta aspayt-**tando***

Can I leave a message with his secretary? Posso lasciare un
messaggio alla sua segretaria?
*pos-so la-**shah**ray oon mays-**sad**-jo al-la soo-a saygray-**tar**-ya*

I am free tomorrow morning/for lunch Sono libero domani
mattina/per pranzo
*sohnoh **lee**-bayro do-**mah**nee mat-**teena**/payr prantso*

Here is my business card Ecco il mio biglietto da visita
*ek-ko eel mee-o beel-**yayt**-to da **vee**-zeeta*

Can I send a telex from here? Posso mandare un telex da
qui?
*pos-so man-**dah**ray oon telex da kwee*

Where can I get some photocopying done? Dove posso far
fare delle fotocopie?
*dohvay pos-so fahr **fah**ray dayl-lay foto-**kop**-yay*

I want to send this by courier Voglio spedire questo tramite
corriere
*vol-yo spay-**dee**ray kwaysto **tra**-meetay kor-ree-e-ray*

I will send you further details/a sample Le manderò
ulteriori dettagli/un campione
*lay manday-**ro** ooltayr-**yoh**ree dayt-**tal**-yee/oon kamp-**yoh**nay*

Have you a catalogue/some literature? Avete un
catalogo/del materiale informativo?
*a-**vay**tay oon kata-logo/del matayr-**yah**lay eenfor-ma-**tee**vo*

I am going to the trade fair/the exhibition Vado alla fiera
commerciale/all'esposizione
*vahdo al-la fee-e-ra kom-mayr-**chah**lay/al-layspo-zeets-**yoh**nay*

See also Colours and shapes, describing things,
measurements and quantities, paying, shopping.

Do you sell stamps? Vende francobolli?
*vaynday frankoh-**bohl**-lee*

How much is that? Quanto costa quello?
kwanto kohsta kwayl-lo

Have you anything smaller/bigger?
Avete qualcosa di più piccolo/di più
grande?
*a-**vay**tay kwal-**ko**za dee pee-oo **peek**-
kolo/dee pee-oo granday*

Have you got any bread/matches?
Avete del pane/dei fiammiferi?
*a-**vay**tay del pahnay/day-ee fee-am-**mee**-
fayree*

I'd like a newspaper/some apples
Vorrei un giornale/delle mele
*vor-**re**-ee oon jor-**nah**lay/dayl-lay maylay*

I prefer this one Preferisco questo
*prayfay-**rees**ko kwaysto*

I'd like to see the one in the window
Vorrei vedere quello in vetrina
*vor-**re**-ee vay-**day**ray kwayl-lo een vay-
treena*

I'll take this one/that one there Prendo
questo/quello là
prendo kwaysto/kwayl-lo la

Could you wrap it up for me please?
Può incartarlo per favore?
*pwo eenkahr-**tahr**lo payr fa-**voh**ray*

**I think you've given me the wrong
change** Penso che abbiate sbagliato a
darmi il resto
*paynso kay ab-**yah**tay zbal-**yah**to a darmee
eel resto*

100 grammes of
un etto di
oon et-to dee

a kilo of
un chilo di
oon keelo dee

cheaper
meno costoso
*mayno koh-
stohzoh*

department
il reparto
*ray-**pahr**to*

**department
store**
il grande
magazzino
*granday magadz-
zeeno*

expensive
costoso
*kohs-**toh**zoh*

shop
il negozio
*nay**gots**-yo*

supermarket
il supermercato
*soopayr-mayr-
kahto*

There are numerous official camping sites with excellent facilities, sometimes including a restaurant and store. Never camp without permission in fields or on common land, as penalties are severe.

We are looking for a campsite Stiamo cercando un campeggio
stee-__ahmo__ chayr-__kando__ oon kamp__payd__-jo

Do you have any vacancies? Avete dei posti liberi?
a-__vaytay__ day-ee pohstee lee-bayree

How much is it per night? Quanto costa per notte?
kwanto kohsta payr not-tay

We want to stay one week Vogliamo restare per una settimana
vol-__yahmo__ rays-__tah__ray payr oona sayt-tee-__mahna__

May we camp here? Possiamo campeggiare qui?
pos-__yahmo__ kampayd-__jah__ray kwee

Is there a more sheltered/secluded site? C'è un posto più riparato/appartato? *che oon pohstoh pee-oo reepa-__rahto__/ap-par-__tahto__*

Can we park our caravan there? Possiamo mettere là la nostra roulotte? *pos-__yahmo__ __mayt__-tayray la la nostra roo__lot__*

Is there a shop/restaurant on the site? C'è uno spaccio/un ristorante nel campeggio?
che oono spat-cho/oon reesto-__rantay__ nayl kampayd-jo

Where is the washroom/drinking water? Dov'è il bagno/l'acqua potabile? *doh__ve__ eel ban-yo/lakwa po__tah__-beelay*

air-mattress il materassino gonfiabile	*matay-ras-__seeno__ gonfee-__ah__-beelay*
camp-bed il lettino da campeggio	*layt-__teeno__ da kampayd-jo*
gas cylinder la bombola di gas	*__bohm__-bohla dee gas*
guy rope il tirante	*tee-__rantay__*
mallet la mazza	*mats-sa*
sleeping bag il sacco a pelo	*sak-ko a paylo*
tent la tenda	*tenda*
tent peg il picchetto	*peekayt-to*
tent pole il palo	*pahlo*
trailer il rimorchio	*reemork-yo*

I want to hire a car to drive myself Voglio noleggiare una macchina per guidare da solo
*vol-yo nolayd-**jah**ray oona **mak**-keena payr gwee-**dah**ray da sohloh*

I need a car with a chauffeur Mi occorre una macchina con autista
*mee ok-**kohr**-ray oona **mak**-keena kohn ow-**teesta***

I want a large/small car Voglio una macchina grande/piccola
*vol-yo oona **mak**-keena granday/**peek**-kola*

Is there a charge per km? Bisogna pagare secondo il chilometraggio?
*beez**ohn**-ya pa-**gah**ray say-**kohn**doh eel keelo-maytrad-jo*

How much extra is the comprehensive insurance cover? Quant'è il supplemento per l'assicurazione che copre tutti i rischi?
*kwan-**te** eel sooplay-**mayn**to payr lasee-koorats-**yoh**nay kay kohpray toot-tee ee reeskee*

I would like to leave the car in Rome Vorrei lasciare la macchina a Roma
*vor-**re**-ee lashahray la **mak**-keena a rohma*

My husband/wife will be driving as well Anche mio marito/mia moglie guiderà
*ankay mee-o ma-**ree**to/mee-a mohl-yay gweeday-**ra***

Is there a radio/radio-cassette? C'è la radio/lo stereo?
*che la **rahd**-yo/lo **ste**-ray-o*

How do I operate the controls? Come funzionano i comandi?
*kohmay foontsee-**oh**-nano ee ko-**man**dee*

Please explain the car documents Per favore mi spieghi i documenti della macchina
*payr fa-**voh**ray mee spee-e-gee ee dokoo-**mayn**tee dayl-la **mak**-keena*

accelerator
un acceleratore
at-chaylay-ra-tohray

alternator
un alternatore
altayr-na-tohray

battery
la batteria
bat-tayree-a

bonnet
il cofano
ko-fano

boot
il portabagagli
porta-bagal-yee

brake fluid
l'olio per i freni
ol-yo payr ee fraynee

brakes
i freni
fraynee

carburettor
il carburatore
kahrboo-ra-tohray

choke
l'aria
ahr-ya

clutch
la frizione
freets-yohnay

distributor
il distributore
deestree-boo-tohray

dynamo
la dinamo
dee-namo

engine
il motore
moh-tohray

exhaust pipe
il tubo di scappamento
toobo dee skap-pa-maynto

fan belt
la cinghia del ventilatore
cheeng-ya dayl vayntee-la-tohray

fuse
il fusibile
foozee-beelay

gears
le marce
mahrchay

handbrake
il freno a mano
frayno a mahno

headlights
i fari anteriori
fahree antayr-yohree

hose
il manicotto
manee-kot-to

ignition
l'accensione
at-chayns-yohnay

indicator
un indicatore
eendee-ka-tohray

points
le puntine
poon-teenay

radiator
il radiatore
rad-ya-tohray

reversing lights
le luci di retromarcia
loochee dee raytro-marcha

shock absorber
un ammortizzatore
am-morteedz-za-tohray

spark plug
la candela
kan-dayla

steering
lo sterzo
stayrtso

steering wheel
il volante
vo-lantay

tyre
la gomma
gohm-ma

wheel
la ruota
rwota

windscreen
il parabrezza
para-braydz-za

windscreen washer
il lavacristallo
lahva-kree-stal-lo

windscreen wiper
il tergicristallo
tayrjee-kree-stal-lo

When are the local festivals? Quando sono le feste locali?
*kwando sohnoh le festay lo-***kah***lee*

Happy birthday! Buon compleanno!
*bwon komplay-***an***-no*

Merry Christmas! Buon Natale!
*bwon na-***tah***lay*

Happy New Year! Buon Anno!
bwon an-no

Congratulations! Felicitazioni!
*faylee-cheetats-***yoh***nee*

Best wishes for ... Tanti auguri per ...
*tantee ow-***goo***ree payr ...*

Have a good time! Buon divertimento!
*bwon deevayr-tee-***mayn***to*

Cheers! Salute!
*sa-***loo***tay*

Enjoy your meal! Buon appetito!
*bwon ap-pay-***tee***to*

baptism
il battesimo
*bat-***tay***-zeemo*

birthday
il compleanno
*komplay-***an***-no*

christening
il battesimo
*bat-***tay***-zeemo*

Christmas
il Natale
*na-***tah***lay*

holiday
la festa
festa

New Year
l'Anno Nuovo
an-no nwovo

party
la festa
festa

public holiday
la festa nazionale
*festa nats-yo-***nah***lay*

wedding
il matrimonio
*matree-***mon***-yo*

**I want something for a headache/a
sore throat/toothache** Voglio qualcosa
per il mal di testa/mal di gola/mal di denti
*vol-yo kwal-koza payr eel mal dee testa/mal
dee gohla/mal dee dentee*

I would like some sticking plaster
Vorrei dei cerotti
vor-re-ee day-ee chayrot-tee

**Have you anything for insect
bites/sunburn/diarrhoea?** Avete
qualcosa per le punture di
insetti/scottature solari/diarrea?
*a-vaytay kwal-koza payr lay poon-tooray
dee eenset-tee/skot-ta-tooray
so-lahree/dee-ar-ray-a*

I have a cold/a cough Ho il raffredore/la
tosse
o eel raf-fray-dohray/la tohs-say

Is this suitable for an upset stomach?
Questo va bene per dei disturbi allo
stomaco?
*kwaysto va benay payr day-ee dee-stoorbee
al-lo sto-mako*

How much/how many do I take?
Quanto/quanti ne devo prendere?
kwanto/kwantee nay dayvo pren-dayray

How often do I take it? Ogni quante ore
devo prenderlo?
on-yee kwantay ohray dayvo pren-dayrlo

How do I get reimbursed? Come si fa
per essere rimborsati?
*kohmay see fa payr es-sayray
reembor-sahtee*

I have a prescription from a doctor Ho
una ricetta dal dottore
o oona reechayt-ta dayl doht-tohray

antiseptic
un antisettico
antee-set-teeko

aspirin
un'aspirina
aspee-reena

bandage
una benda
benda

chemist's
la farmacia
farma-chee-a

contraceptive
il contraccettivo
kontrat-chayt-teevo

cotton wool
il cotone idrofilo
koh-tohnay ee-dro-feelo

cream
la crema
kre-ma

insect repellent
un insettifugo
eensayt-tee-foogo

laxative
il lassativo
las-sa-teevo

lotion
la lozione
lohts-yohnay

sanitary towels
gli assorbenti
as-sor-bayntee

tampons
le tamponi
tam-pohnee

I have a small baby/two children Ho un bambino piccolo/due bambini
o oon bam-beeno peek-kolo/doo-ay bam-beenee

Do you have a special rate for children? Avete delle riduzioni per bambini?
a-vaytay dayl-lay reeduts-yohnee payr bam-beenee

Do you have facilities/activities for children? Avete dei servizi/organizzate delle attività per bambini?
a-vaytay day-ee sayr-veetsee/orga-needz-zahtay dayl-lay at-teevee-ta payr bam-beenee

Have you got a cot for the baby? Avete un lettino per il bambino?
a-vaytay oon layt-teeno payr eel bam-beeno

Where can I feed/change the baby? Dove posso allattare/cambiare il bambino?
dohvay pos-so al-lat-tahray/kamb-yahray eel bam-beeno

Where can I warm the baby's bottle? Dove posso riscaldare il biberon?
dohvay pos-so reeskal-dahray eel beebay-ron

Is there a playroom? C'è una stanza giochi?
che oona stantsa jokee

Is there a babysitting service? C'è un servizio di babysitter?
che oon sayr-veets-yo dee babysitter

My daughter is nine and my son is six Mia figlia ha nove anni e mio figlio ne ha sei
mee-a feel-ya a nohvay an-nee ay mee-o feel-yo nay a se-ee

---

baby food
gli alimenti per bambini
alee-mayntee payr bam-beenee

babysitter
baby-sitter
baby-sitter

boy
il bambino
bam-beeno

child
il bambino
bam-beeno

disposable nappies
i pannolini da buttar via
pan-no-leenee da boot-tar vee-a

dummy
la tettarella
tayt-ta-rel-la

girl
la bambina
bam-beena

high chair
il seggiolone
sayd-joh-lohnay

nappies
i pannolini per bambini
pan-no-leenee payr bam-beenee

pram
la carrozzina
kar-rots-seena

push chair
il passeggino
pas-sayd-jeeno

Where is the nearest church? Dov'è la chiesa più vicina?
dohve la kee-e-za pee-oo vee-cheena

Where is there a Protestant church? Dove posso trovare una chiesa protestante?
dohvay pos-so tro-vahray oona kee-e-za protay-stantay

I want to see a priest Voglio vedere un prete
vol-yo vay-dayray oon pre-tay

What time is the service? A che ora è la messa?
a kay ohra e la mays-sa

I want to go to confession Voglio andare a confessarmi
vol-yo an-dahray a konfays-sahrmee

altar
un altare
al-tahray

candle
la candela
kan-dayla

cathedral
la cattedrale
kat-tay-drahlay

Catholic
cattolico
kat-to-leeko

chapel
la cappella
kap-pel-la

churchyard
il cimitero di una chiesa
cheemee-tayro dee oona kee-e-za

mass
la messa
mays-sa

minister
il sacerdote
sachayr-dotay

mosque
la moschea
mos-kay-a

rabbi
il rabbino
rab-beeno

synagogue
la sinagoga
seena-goga

Does this bus/train go to ...?
Quest'autobus/treno va a ...?
kwaystow-toboos/treno va a ...

Which number bus goes to ...? Quale
autobus va a ...?
kwahlay ow-toboos va a ...

**Where do I get a bus for the
airport/cathedral?** Da dove parte
l'autobus per l'aeroporto/il duomo?
*da dohvay partay low-toboos payr la-ayro-
porto/eel dwomo*

Which bus do I take for the museum?
Quale autobus devo prendere per andare al
museo?
*kwahlay ow-toboos dayvo pren-dayray payr
an-dahray al mooze-o*

Where do I change/get off? Dove devo
cambiare/scendere?
dohvay dayvo kamb-yahray/shayn-dayray

**How frequent are the buses/trains to
town?** Ogni quanto ci sono gli autobus/i
treni per la città?
*on-yee kwanto chee sohnoh lyee ow-
toboos/ee trenee payr la cheet-ta*

What is the fare to the town centre?
Qual'è la tariffa per andare in centro?
*kwahle la tareef-fa payr an-dahray een
chentro*

Where do I buy a ticket? Dove posso
comprare il biglietto?
*dohvay pos-so kom-prahray eel beel-yayt-
to*

What time is the last bus? Quando
parte l'ultimo autobus?
kwando partay lool-teemo ow-toboos

book of tickets
il blocchetto di
biglietti
*blok-kayt-to dee
beel-yayt-tee*

bus stop
la fermata
dell'autobus
*fayr-mahta dayl-
low-toboos*

conductor
il bigliettaio
beel-yayt-ta-yo

driver
un autista
ow-teesta

escalator
la scala mobile
skahla mo-beelay

half fare
metà prezzo
mayta prets-so

lift
un ascensore
ashayn-sohray

season ticket
un abbonamento
ab-bona-maynto

tourist ticket
il biglietto turistico
*beel-yayt-to
tooree-steeko*

underground
la metropolitana
maytro-polee-tahna

Is there a laundry service? C'è un
servizio di lavanderia?
che oon sayrveets-yo dee lavan-dayree-a

**Is there a launderette/dry cleaner's
nearby?** C'è una lavanderia
automatica/lavanderia a secco qui vicino?
*che oona lavan-dayree-a owto-ma-
teeka/lavan-dayree-a a sayk-ko kwee vee-
cheeno*

**Where can I get this skirt
cleaned/ironed?** Dove posso far
pulire/stirare questa gonna?
*dohvay pos-so fahr poo-leeray/stee-rahray
kwysta gon-na*

Where can I do some washing? Dove
posso fare del bucato?
dohvay pos-so fahray dayl boo-kahto

I need some soap and water Mi occorre
acqua e sapone
mee ohk-kohr-ray akwa ay sa-pohnay

Where can I dry my clothes? Dove
posso far asciugare i vestiti?
*dohvay pos-so fahr ashoo-gahray ee vay-
steetee*

This stain is coffee Questa è una macchia
di caffè
kwysta e oona mak-ya dee kaf-fe

Can you remove this stain? Può
smacchiare questo?
pwo zmak-yahray kwysto

This fabric is very delicate Questa
stoffa è molto delicata
kwysta stof-fa e mohltoh daylee-kahta

When will my things be ready?
Quando saranno pronte le mie cose?
kwando saran-no prontay lay mee-ay kozay

disinfectant	il disinfettante *deezeen-fayt-tantay*
laundry room	la lavanderia *lavan-day-ree-a*
sink	il lavandino *lavan-deeno*
tap	il rubinetto *roobee-nayt-to*
to dry	asciugare *ashoo-gahray*
to wash	lavare *la-vahray*
washbasin	la bacinella *bachee-nayl-la*
washing powder	il detersivo *daytayr-seevo*
washroom	il bagno *ban-yo*

I take a continental size 40 Porto la misura 40
porto la mee-zoora kwa-ranta

Can you measure me please? Può prendermi le misure?
pwo pren-dermee lay mee-zooray

May I try on this dress? Posso provare questo vestito?
pos-so pro-vahray kwaysto vay-steeto

May I take it over to the light? Posso vederlo alla luce?
pos-so vay-dayrlo al-la loochay

Where are the changing rooms? Dove sono gli spogliatoi?
dohvay sohnoh lyee spolyah-to-ee

Is there a mirror? C'è uno specchio?
che oono spek-yo

It's too big/small È troppo grande/piccolo
e trop-po granday/peek-kolo

What is the material? Che stoffa è?
kay stof-fa e

Is it washable? È lavabile?
e lavah-beelay

I don't like it/them Non mi piace/piacciono
nohn mee pee-achay/pee-at-chono

I don't like the colour Non mi piace il colore
nohn mee pee-achay eel koh-lohray

belt
la cintura
cheen-toora

blouse
la camicetta
kamee-chayt-ta

bra
il reggiseno
rayd-jee-sayno

button
il bottone
boht-tohnay

cardigan
il cardigan
cardigan

clothes
i vestiti
vay-steetee

coat
il cappotto
kap-pot-to

cotton
il cotone
koh-tohnay

denim
stoffa di jeans
stof-fa dee jeans

dress
il vestito
vay-steeto

fabric
la stoffa
stof-fa

fur
la pelliccia
payl-leet-cha

cont.

gloves
i guanti
gwantee

hat
il cappello
kap-pel-lo

jacket
la giacca
jak-ka

jeans
i jeans
jeans

lace
il pizzo
peets-so

leather
il cuoio
kwo-yo

nightdress
la camicia da notte
ka-meecha da not-tay

nylon
il nylon
nylon

panties
le mutandine
mootan-deenay

pants
le mutande
moo-tanday

petticoat
la sottogonna
sot-togon-na

polyester
il poliestere
polee-e-stayray

pyjamas
i pigiama
pee-jama

raincoat
un impermeabile
eempayr-may-ah-beelay

sandals
i sandali
san-dalee

scarf
la sciarpa
shahrpa

shirt
la camicia
ka-meecha

shoes
le scarpe
skahrpay

shorts
i calzoncini corti
kaltson-cheenee kortee

silk
la seta
seta

skirt
la gonna
gon-na

socks
i calzini
kalt-seenee

stockings
le calze
kaltsay

suede
il camoscio
ka-mosho

suit (man's)
un abito
a-beeto

suit (woman's)
il tailleur
ta-yer

sweater
il maglione
mal-yohnay

swimsuit
il costume da bagno
ko-stoomay da ban-yo

t-shirt
la maglietta
mal-yayt-ta

tie
la cravatta
kravat-ta

tights
i collant
kol-lan

trousers
i pantaloni
panta-lohnee

trunks
i calzoncini da bagno
kaltson-cheenee da ban-yo

vest
la canottiera
kanot-yera

wool
la lana
lana

zip
la cerniera
chayrn-ye-ra

Is there a bus to ...? C'è un autobus
per ...?
*che oon **ow**-toboos payr ...*

Which bus goes to ...? Quale autobus
va a ...?
*kwahlay **ow**-toboos va a ...*

Where do I catch the bus for ...? Dove
posso prendere l'autobus per ...?
*dohvay pos-so **pren**-dayray low-toboos
payr ...*

What are the times of the buses to ...?
Quando partono gli autobus per ...?
*kwando **pahr**-tono lyee **ow**-toboos payr ...*

Does this bus go to ...? Quest'autobus va
a ...?
*kway**stow**-toboos va a ...*

Where do I get off? Dove devo scendere?
*dohvay dayvo **shayn**-dayray*

Is there a toilet on board? C'è una
toilette sull'autobus?
*che oona twa**let** sool-**low**-toboos*

Is there an overnight service to ...? C'è
un servizio notturno per ...?
*che oon sayr-**veets**-yo not-**toorno** payr...*

What time does it leave/arrive? A che
ora parte/arriva?
*a kay ohra partay/ar-**reeva***

Will you tell me where to get off? Mi
può dire quando devo scendere?
*mee pwo deeray kwando dayvo **shayn**-
dayray*

Let me off here please Mi faccia
scendere qui per favore
*mee fat-cha **shayn**-dayray kwee payr fa-
vohray*

bus depot
il deposito degli
autobus
*daypo-zeeto dayl-
lyee **ow**-toboos*

driver
un autista
*ow-**teesta***

film show
il film
feelm

luggage hold
il bagagliaio
*bagal-**ya**-yo*

luggage rack
il portabagagli
*porta-bag**al**-yee*

seat
il sedile
*say-**deelay***

beige
beige
bej

big
grande
granday

black
nero
nayro

blue
blu
blu

brown
marrone
mar-rohnay

circular
circolare
cheerko-lahray

crimson
color cremisi
kohlohr kray-meezee

cube
cubo
koobo

dark
scuro
skooro

fat
grasso
gras-so

flat
piatto
pee-at-to

gold
color oro
kohlor oroh

green
verde
vayrday

grey
grigio
greejo

lemon
color limone
kohlohr lee-mohnay

light
chiaro
kee-aro

long
lungo
loongo

mauve
color malva
kohlohr malva

oblong
oblungo
ob-loongo

orange
arancione
aran-chohnay

oval
ovale
o-vahlay

pink
rosa
roza

pointed
appuntito
ap-poon-teeto

purple
viola
vee-ola

red
rosso
ros-so

round
rotondo
roh-tohndo

shade
tonalità
tona-leeta

shiny
lucido
loo-cheedo

silver
color argento
kohlor ar-jaynto

small
piccolo
peek-kolo

square
quadrato
kwad-rahto

thick
spesso
spays-so

thin
magro
magro

turquoise
turchese
toor-kayzay

white
bianco
bee-anko

yellow
giallo
jal-lo

This does not work Questo non funziona
kwaysto nohn foonts-yohna

I can't turn the heating off/on Non riesco a spegnere ad
accendere il riscaldimento
*nohn ree-esko a spayn-yayray/ad at-chen-dayray eel
reeskal-dee-maynto*

The lock is broken La serratura è rotta
la sayr-ra-toora è roht-ta

I can't open the window Non riesco ad aprire la finestra
nohn ree-esko ad a-preeray la fee-nestra

The toilet won't flush Non esce acqua dal water
nohn e-shay ak-kwa dal vatayr

There is no hot water/toilet paper Non c'è acqua calda/carta
igienica
nohn che ak-kwa kalda/kahrta ee-je-neeka

The washbasin is dirty Il lavandino è sporco
eel lavan-deeno e sporko

The room is noisy La stanza è rumorosa
la stantsa e roomoh-rohza

My coffee is cold Il caffè è freddo
eel kaf-fe è fred-do

We are still waiting to be served Stiamo ancora aspettando
di essere serviti
stee-ahmo an-kohra aspayt-tando dee es-sayray sayr-veetee

I bought this here yesterday Questo l'ho comprato qui ieri
kwaysto lo kom-prahto kwee ye-ree

It has a flaw/hole in it È difettoso/bucato
e deefayt-tohzo/boo-kahto

See also GREETINGS.

How do you do?/Hello/Goodbye Piacere!/Buon
giorno/Arrivederci
pee-a-chayray/bwon jorno/ar-reevay-dayrchee

May I introduce myself? Permetta che mi presenti
payr-mayt-ta kay mee pray-zayntee

Do you speak English? Parla inglese?
parla een-glayzay

I don't speak Italian Non parlo italiano
nohn parlo eetal-yahno

What's your name? Come si chiama?
kohmay see kee-ahma

My name is ... Mi chiamo ...
mee kee-ahmo ...

Do you mind if I sit here? Le dispiace se mi siedo qui?
lay deespee-achay say mee see-e-do kwee

I'm English/Irish/Scottish/Welsh Sono
inglese/irlandese/scozzese/gallese
sohnoh een-glayzay/eerlan-dayzay/skots-sayzay/gal-layzay

Are you Italian? Lei è italiano?
le-ee e eetal-yahno

Where do you come from? Da dove viene?
da dohvay vee-e-nay

Would you like a cup of coffee/a drink? Gradisce un
caffè/qualcosa da bere?
gra-deeshay oon kaf-fe/kwal-koza da bayray

Would you like to come out with me? Vuole uscire con me?
vwolay oo-sheeray kohn may

Yes, I should like to Sì, volentieri
see volaynt-ye-ree

No, thank you No, grazie
no grats-yay

Yes please/No thank you Sì grazie/No grazie
see grats-yay/no grats-yay

Thank you (very much) (Molte) grazie
(mohltay) grats-yay

Don't mention it Prego
praygo

I'm sorry Mi dispiace
mee deespee-achay

I'm on holiday here Sono qui in vacanza
sohnoh kwee een vakant-sa

This is my first trip to ... Questo è il mio primo viaggio a ...
kwaysto e eel mee-o preemo vee-ad-jo a ...

Do you mind if I smoke? Le dispiace se fumo?
lay deespee-achay say foomo

Would you like a drink? Vuole qualcosa da bere?
vwolay kwal-koza da bayray

Have you ever been to Britain? È mai stato in Gran
Bretagna?
e ma-ee stahto een gran braytan-ya

Did you like it there? Le è piaciuto?
lay e pee-a-chooto

What part of Italy are you from? Da quale parte dell'Italia
viene?
dah kwahlay partay del-leetal-ya vee-e-nay

In the weight and length charts, the middle figure can be either metric or imperial. Thus 3.3 feet=1 metre, 1 foot=0.3 metres, and so on.

feet		metres	inches		cm	lbs		kg
3.3	1	0.3	0.39	1	2.54	2.2	1	0.45
6.6	2	0.61	0.79	2	5.08	4.4	2	0.91
9.9	3	0.91	1.18	3	7.62	6.6	3	1.4
13.1	4	1.22	1.57	4	10.6	8.8	4	1.8
16.4	5	1.52	1.97	5	12.7	11	5	2.2
19.7	6	1.83	2.36	6	15.2	13.2	6	2.7
23	7	2.13	2.76	7	17.8	15.4	7	3.2
26.2	8	2.44	3.15	8	20.3	17.6	8	3.6
29.5	9	2.74	3.54	9	22.9	19.8	9	4.1
32.9	10	3.05	3.9	10	25.4	22	10	4.5
			4.3	11	27.9			
			4.7	12	30.1			

°C	0	5	10	15	17	20	22	24	26	28	30	35	37	38	40	50	100
°F	32	41	50	59	63	68	72	75	79	82	86	95	98.4	100	104	122	212

Km	10	20	30	40	50	60	70	80	90	100	110	120
Miles	6.2	12.4	18.6	24.9	31	37.3	43.5	49.7	56	62	68.3	74.6

Tyre pressures

lb/sq in	15	18	20	22	24	26	28	30	33	35
kg/sq cm	1.1	1.3	1.4	1.5	1.7	1.8	2	2.1	2.3	2.5

Liquids

gallons	1.1	2.2	3.3	4.4	5.5	pints	0.44	0.88	1.76
litres	5	10	15	20	25	litres	0.25	0.5	1

I have nothing to declare Non ho niente da dichiarare
nohn o nee-entay da deek-ya-rahray

I have the usual allowances of alcohol/tobacco Ho la
quantità consentita di alcool/tabacco
o la kwantee-ta konsayn-teeta dee alko-ol/tabak-ko

I have two bottles of wine/a bottle of spirits to declare
Ho due bottiglie di vino/una bottiglia di liquore da dichiarare
o doo-ay bot-teel-yay dee veeno/oona bot-teel-ya dee lee-kwohray da deek-ya-rahray

My wife/husband and I have a joint passport Io e mia
moglie/ mio marito siamo sullo stesso passaporto
ee-oh ay mee-a mol-yay/mee-o ma-reeto see-ahmo sool-lo stays-so pas-sa-porto

The chidren are on this passport I bambini sono su questo
passaporto
ee bam-beenee sohnoh soo kwaysto pas-sa-porto

I am a British national Sono di nazionalità britannica
sohnoh dee nats-yoh-nalee-ta breetan-neeka

I shall be staying in this country for three weeks Resterò
in questo paese per tre settimane
raystayro een kwaysto pa-ayzay payr tray sayt-tee-mahnay

We are here on holiday Siamo qui in vacanza
see-ahmo kwee een va-kantsa

I am here on business Sono qui per affari
sohnoh kwee payr af-fahree

I have an entry visa Ho un visto di entrata
o oon veesto dee ayn-trahta

See also NUMBERS

What is the date today?	Che giorno è oggi?
	kay jorno eh od-jee
It's the ...	È il ... *eh eel*

1st of March	**2nd of June**
primo marzo	il due giugno
preemo martso	*eel doo-ay joon-yo*

We will arrive on the 29th of August Arriveremo il 29 agosto
arree-vay-raymo eel ventee-novay agos-to

1984 millenovecentoottantaquattro
meel-laynovay-chento ot-tanta-kwat-tro

Monday	lunedì	*loonay-dee*
Tuesday	martedì	*martay-dee*
Wednesday	mercoledì	*mayrko-laydee*
Thursday	giovedì	*jovay-dee*
Friday	venerdì	*vaynayr-dee*
Saturday	sabato	*sa-bato*
Sunday	domenica	*domay-neeka*

January	**May**	**September**
gennaio	maggio	settembre
jen-na-yo	*mad-jo*	*set-tembray*
February	**June**	**October**
febbraio	giugno	ottobre
feb-bra-yo	*joon-yo*	*ot-tohbray*
March	**July**	**November**
marzo	luglio	novembre
martso	*lool-yo*	*novem-bray*
April	**August**	**December**
aprile	agohsto	dicembre
apreelay	*agohs-to*	*deechem-bray*

See also DOCTOR (1).

I need to see the dentist (urgently) Devo farmi vedere dal
dentista (urgentemente)
dayvo fahrmee vay-dayray dal dayn-teesta (oorjayn-tay-mayntay)

I have toothache Ho mal di denti
o mal dee dentee

I've broken a tooth Mi sono spezzato un dente
mee sohnoh spayts-sahto oon dentay

A filling has come out Mi è uscita l'otturazione
mee e oo-sheeta lot-toorats-yohnay

My gums are bleeding/are sore Mi esce sangue dalle
gengive/Mi fanno male le gengive
*mee eshay sangwe dal-lay jayn-jeevay/mee fan-no mahlay lay
jayn-jeevay*

Please give me an injection Mi faccia un'iniezione per favore
mee fat-cha ooneen-yets-yohnay payr fa-vohray

My dentures need repairing La mia dentiera deve essere
riparata
la mee-a daynt-ye-ra dayvay es-sayray reepa-rahta

THE DENTIST MAY SAY:

Devo fare un'estrazione
dayvo fahray oonay-strats-yohnay
I shall have to take it out

Le occorre un'otturazione
lay ok-kohr-ray oonot-toorats-yohnay
You need a filling

Questo le potrà fare un pò male
kwaysto lay potra fahray oon po mahlay
This might hurt a bit

bad
cattivo
kat-teevo

beautiful
bello
bel-lo

bitter
acido
a-cheedo

clean
pulito
poo-leeto

cold
freddo
frayd-do

difficult
difficile
deef-fee-cheelay

dirty
sporco
sporko

easy
facile
fa-cheelay

excellent
ottimo
ot-teemoh

far
lontano
lon-tahno

fast
veloce
vay-lohchay

good
buono
bwono

hard
duro
dooro

heavy
pesante
pay-zantay

horrible
orribile
or-ree-beelay

hot
caldo
kaldo

interesting
interessante
eentay-rays-santay

light
leggero
layd-je-ro

long
lungo
loongo

lovely
piacevole
pee-achay-volay

near
vicino
vee-cheeno

new
nuovo
nwovo

old
vecchio
vayk-yo

pleasant
gradevole
graday-volay

rough
ruvido
roo-veedo

short
corto
korto

slow
lento
laynto

smooth
liscio
leesho

soft
soffice
sof-feechay

sour
aspro
aspro

spicy
piccante
peek-kantay

strong
forte
fortay

sweet
dolce
dohlchay

unpleasant
sgradevole
zgraday-volay

warm
caldo
kaldo

weak
debole
day-bolay

See also MAPS AND GUIDES.
To attract someone's attention, you should preface your
question with *Scusi* (Excuse me).

Where is the nearest post office? Dov'è
l'ufficio postale più vicino?
doh-ve loof-feecho po-stahlay pee-oo vee-cheeno

How do I get to the airport? Come
faccio per andare all'aeroporto?
kohmay fat-cho payr an-dahray al-la-ayro-porto

Can you tell me the way to ...? Può
indicarmi la strada per ...?
pwo eendee-kahrmee la strahda payr ...?

Is this the right way to the cathedral?
È questa la strada che va al duomo?
e kwaysta la strahda kay va al dwomo

**I am looking for the tourist
information office** Sto cercando
l'ufficio informazioni turistiche
sto chayr-kando loof-feecho eenfor-mats-yohnee too-reesteekay

Which road do I take for ...? Quale
strada devo prendere per ...?
kwahlay strahda dayvo pren-dayray payr ...

Is this the turning for ...? Devo girare
qui per ...?
dayvo jeerah-ray kwee payr ...

How do I get on to the motorway?
Come faccio per entrare nell'autostrada?
kohmay fat-cho payr ayn-trahray nayl-lowto-strahda

How long will it take to get there?
Quanto tempo ci vuole per arrivarci?
kwanto tempo chee vwolay payr ar-ree-vahrchee

corner	un angolo
	an-golo
far	lontano
	lon-tahno
left	sinistra
	see-neestra
near	vicino
	vee-cheeno
over	sopra
	sohpra
over there	là
	la
right	destra
	destra
road signs	i segnali stradali
	sayn-yahlee stra-dahlee
straight on	diritto
	deereet-to
through	attraverso
	at-tra-vayrso
under	sotto
	soht-to

See also BODY.

Medical advice and treatment are available to British and Irish visitors on the same basis as for Italian subjects. In order to make sure you are treated free of charge, you should take with you form E111, issued by the DHSS.

I need a doctor Ho bisogno di un dottore
o beezohn-yo dee oon doht-tohray

Can I make an appointment with the doctor? Posso avere un appuntamento con il dottore?
pos-so a-vayray oon ap-poonta-maynto kohn eel doht-tohray

My wife is ill Mia moglie sta male
mee-a mol-yay sta mahlay

I have a sore throat/a stomach upset Ho mal dee gola/dei disturbi allo stomaco
o mal dee gohla/day-ee dee-stoorbee al-lo sto-mako

He has diarrhoea/earache Ha la diarrea/il mal d'orecchio
a la dee-ar-ray-a/eel mal dorek-yo

I am constipated Sono stitico
sohnoh stee-teeko

I have a pain here/in my chest Ho un dolore qui/al petto
o oon doh-lohray kwee/al pet-to

She has a temperature Ha la febbre
a la feb-bray

He has been stung/bitten È stato punto/morso
e stahto poonto/morso

He can't breathe/walk Non può respirare/camminare
nohn pwo rayspee-rahray/kam-mee-nahray

I feel dizzy Ho il capogiro
o eel kapo-jeero

cough
la tosse
tohs-say

cut
il taglio
tal-yo

faint, to
svenire
zvay-neeray

food poisoning
un'intossicazione alimentare
eentos-seekats-yohnay alee-mayn-tahray

hay fever
la febbre da fieno
feb-bray da fee-e-no

headache
il mal di testa
mal dee testa

ill
malato
ma-lahto

I can't sleep/swallow Non riesco a
dormire/ad inghiottire
*nohn ree-esko a dor-meeray/ad eeng-yot-
teeray*

She has been sick Ha vomitato
a vomee-tahto

I am diabetic/pregnant Sono
diabetico/incinta
sohnoh dee-a-be-teeko/een-cheenta

I am allergic to penicillin/cortisone
Sono allergico alla penicillina/al cortisone
*sohnoh al-layr-geeko al-la paynee-cheel-
leena/al kortee-zohnay*

I have high blood pressure Ho la
pressione alta
o la prays-yohnay alta

**My blood group is A positive/O
negative** Il mio gruppo sanguigno è A
positivo/O negativo
*eel mee-o groop-po sangween-yo e a
pozee-teevo/o nayga-teevo*

THE DOCTOR MAY SAY:

Deve restare a letto
dayvay ray-stahray a let-to
You must stay in bed

Deve andare in ospedale
dayvay an-dahray een ospay-dahlay
You will have to go to hospital

Dovrà subire un intervento
dovra soo-beeray oon eentayr-vaynto
You will need an operation

Prenda questo tre volte al giorno
prenda kwaysto tray voltay al jorno
Take this three times a day

inflamed
infiammato
eenf-yam-mahto

injection
un'iniezione
een-yayts-yohnay

medicine
la medicina
maydee-cheena

painful
doloroso
dohloh-rohzoh

pill
la pillola
peel-lola

poisoning
un'intossicazione
*eentos-seekats-
yohnay*

runny nose
il naso che cola
nahzo kay kohla

tablet
la pastiglia
pasteel-ya

unconscious
svenuto
zvay-nooto

See also WINES AND SPIRITS.

A black/white coffee, please Un
caffè/un cappuccino per favore
*oon kaf-**fe**/oon kap-poot-**chee**no payr fa-
vohray*

Two cups of tea Due tazze di tè
doo-ay tat-say dee te

A pot of tea Un tè per due
oon te payr doo-ay

A glass of lemonade Un bicchiere di
limonata
*oon beek-**ye**-ray dee leemo-**nah**ta*

A bottle of mineral water Una bottiglia
di acqua minerale
*oona bot-**teel**-ya dee akwa meenay-**rah**lay*

Do you have ...? Avete ...?
*a-**vay**tay ...*

Another coffee, please Un altro caffè per
favore
*oon altro kaf-**fe** payr fa-**voh**ray*

A draught beer Una birra alla spina
oona beer-ra al-la speena

With ice please Con ghiaccio per favore
*kohn gee-**at**-cho payr fa-**voh**ray*

beer
la birra
beer-ra

coke
la coca cola
koka kola

**drinking
chocolate**
la cioccolata
*chok-ko-**lah**ta*

drinking water
acqua potabile
*akwa po**tah**-beelay*

fruit juice
il succo di frutta
*sook-ko dee froot-
ta*

lemon tea
tè al limone
*te al lee-**moh**nay*

lemonade
la limonata
*leemo-**nah**ta*

milk
il latte
lat-tay

shandy
la birra con gassosa
*beer-ra kohn gas-
sohza*

soft drink
un analcolico
*anal-**ko**-leekoh*

See also ACCIDENTS - CARS, BREAKDOWNS, CAR PARTS, PETROL STATION, POLICE, ROAD SIGNS.

What is the speed limit on this road?
Qual'è il limite di velocità su questa strada?
kwah-le eel lee-metay dee vaylo-cheeta soo kwaysta strahda

Is there a toll on this motorway? C'è da pagare il pedaggio su questa autostrada?
che da pa-gahray eel pay-dad-jo soo kwaysta owto-strahda

What is causing this hold-up? Perché c'è questo ingorgo?
payrkay che kwaysto een-gohrgo

Is there a short-cut? C'è una scorciatoia?
che oona skorcha-to-ya

Where can I park? Dove posso parcheggiare?
dohvay pos-so parkayd-jahray

Is there a car park nearby? C'è un parcheggio qui vicino?
che oon par-ked-jo kwee vee-cheeno

Can I park here? Posso parcheggiare qui?
pos-so parkayd-jahray kwee

How long can I stay here? Quanto tempo posso restare qui?
kwanto tempo pos-so rays-tahray kwee

Do I need a parking disk? È necessario il disco orario?
e nechays-sahr-yo eel deesko o-rahr-yo

Are seat belts compulsory? Sono obbligatorie le cinture di sicurezza?
Sohnoh ob-bleega-tohree-ay lay cheen-tooray dee seekoo-rayts-sa

bend
la curva
koorva

driving licence
la patente
pa-tentay

major road
la strada principale
strahda preenchee-pahlay

minor road
la strada secondaria
strahda saykon-dahr-ya

motorway
un'autostrada
owto-strahda

one-way
il senso unico
senso oo-neeko

parking meter
il parchimetro
pahr-keemaytro

parking ticket
la contravvenzione
kontrav-vaynts-yohnay

sign
il segnale
sayn-yahlay

traffic lights
il semaforo
saymah-foro

See also DRINKS, FOOD, ORDERING, PAYING.
Trattorie offer excellent food at lower prices than *ristoranti*, and
set-price menus are often good value. Beware of *menu turistici* in
places obviously catering for tourists.

Is there a restaurant/café near here?
C'è un ristorante/un caffè qui vicino?
*che oon reesto-rantay/oon kaf-fe kwee
vee-cheeno*

**We want to find somewhere cheap for
lunch** Vogliamo pranzare in un posto
poco costoso
*vol-yahmo prant-sahray een oon pohstoh
poko koh-stohzoh*

A table for four please Un tavolo per
quattro per favore
oon tah-volo payr kwat-tro payr fa-vohray

May we see the menu? Possiamo vedere
il menu?
pos-yahmo vay-dayray eel menoo

We'd like a drink first Prima prendiamo
qualcosa da bere
preema prend-yahmo kwal-koza da bayray

Could we have some more water?
Possiamo avere altra acqua?
pos-yahmo a-vayray altra akwa

**We'd like a dessert/some mineral
water** Vorremmo un dolce/dell'acqua
minerale
*vor-raym-mo oon dohlchay/del-lakwa
meenay-rahlay*

The bill, please Il conto, per favore
eel kohntoh payr fa-vohray

Is service included? Il servizio è
compreso nel prezzo?
*eel sayr-veets-yo e kom-prayzo nayl
prets-so*

café	il caffè
	kaf-fe
cheese	il formaggio
	formad-jo
dessert	il dolce
	dohlchay
main course	il primo piatto
	preemo pee-at-to
menu	il menu
	maynoo
restaurant	il ristorante
	reesto-rantay
sandwich	il panino
	pa-neeno
soup	la minestra
	mee-nestra
starter	un antipasto
	antee-pasto
terrace	la terrazza
	tayr-rats-sa
vegetables	le verdure
	vayr-dooray

See also ACCIDENTS, BREAKDOWNS, DENTIST, DOCTOR.

There's a fire! C'è un incendio!
che oon een-chend-yo

Call a doctor/an ambulance! Chiamate un dottore/un'ambulanza!
kee-a-mahtay oon doht-tohray/oon amboo-lantsa

We must get him to hospital Dobbiamo portarlo all'ospedale
dob-yahmo por-tarlo al-lospay-dahlay

Fetch help quickly! Andate a chiedere aiuto, presto!
an-dahtay a kee-e-dayray a-yooto presto

He can't swim Non sa nuotare
nohn sa nwo-tahray

Get the police! Chiamate la polizia!
kee-a-mahtay la poleet-see-a

Where's the nearest police station/hospital? Dov'è il posto di polizia/ospedale più vicino?
dohve eel pohstoh dee poleet-see-a/ospay-dahlay pee-oo vee-cheeno

I've lost my credit card Ho perso la mia carta di credito
o payrso la mee-a karta dee kray-deeto

My child/handbag is missing Ho perso mio figlio/la mia borsa
o payrso mee-o feel-yo/la mee-a borsa

My passport/watch has been stolen Mi hanno rubato il passaporto/l'orologio
mee an-no roo-bahto eel pas-sa-porto/lohroh-lojoh

I've forgotten my ticket/my key Ho dimenticato il biglietto/le chiavi
o deemayn-tee-kahto eel beel-yayt-to/lay kee-avee

coastguard
il guardacosta
gwahrda-kosta

consulate
il consolato
konso-lahto

embassy
un'ambasciata
amba-shahta

fire brigade
i vigili del fuoco
vee-jeelee dayl fwoko

fire!
incendio!
eenchaynd-yo

help!
aiuto!
a-yooto

lost property office
un ufficio oggetti smarriti
oof-feecho ohd-jet-tee zmar-reetee

police station
il posto di polizia
pohstoh de poleet-see-a

police!
polizia!
poleet-see-a

stop thief!
fermate il ladro!
fayr-mahtay eel ladro

See also SIGHTSEEING, SPORTS, NIGHTLIFE.

Are there any local festivals? Ci sono
delle feste locali?
*chee sohnoh dayl-lay festay lo-**kah**lee*

**Can you recommend something for
the children?** Può suggerire qualcosa per
i bambini?
*pwo sood-jay-**ree**ray kwal-**ko**za payr ee
bam-**bee**nee*

What is there to do in the evenings?
Che cosa si può fare di sera?
kay koza say pwo fahray dee sayra

Where is there a cinema/theatre?
Dov'è un cinema/teatro?
*dohve oon **chee**-nayma/tay-**ah**tro*

Where can we go to a concert? Dove
possiamo andare per un concerto?
*dohvay pos-**yah**mo an-**dah**ray payr oon
kon-**chayr**to*

Can you book the tickets for us? Può
prenotarci i biglietti?
*pwo prayno-**tahr**chee ee beel-**yayt**-tee*

Is there a swimming pool? C'è una
piscina?
*che oona pee-**shee**na*

Do you know any interesting walks? Ci
sono delle belle passeggiate da fare?
*chee sohnoh dayl-lay bel-lay pas-sayd-
jahtay da fahray*

Where can we play tennis/golf? Dove
possiamo giocare a tennis/a golf?
*dohvay pos-**yah**mo jo-**kah**ray a tennis/a
golf*

admission charge	il prezzo d'entrata *prets-so dayn-trahta*
bar	il bar *bar*
booking office	la biglietteria *beel-yayt-tayree-a*
buffet	il buffet *boo-fe*
club	il club *kloob*
fun fair	il luna park *loona park*
jazz	il jazz *jazz*
orchestra	un'orchestra *or-kaystra*
play	la rappresentazione teatrale *rap-prayzayn-tats-yohnay tay-a-trahlay*
show	lo spettacolo *spayt-tah-kolo*
ticket	il biglietto *beel-yayt-to*

What time is the next sailing? Quando parte la prossima nave?
kwando partay la pros-seema nahvay

A return ticket for one car and two adults and two children Un biglietto di andata e ritorno per una macchina, due adulti e due bambini
oon beel-yayt-to dee an-dahta ay reetorno payr oona mak-keena doo-ay a-dooltee ay doo-ay bam-beenee

How long does the crossing take? Quanto dura la traversata?
kwanto doora la travayr-sahta

Are there any cabins/reclining seats? Ci sono delle cabine/poltrone reclinabili?
chee sohnoh dayl-lay ka-beenay/poltrohnay rayklee-nah-beelee

Is there a TV lounge/bar? C'è una sala TV/un bar?
che oona sahla teevoo/oon bar

Where are the toilets? Dov'è la toilette?
dohve la twalet

Where is the duty-free shop? Dov'è il duty-free?
dohve eel duty free

Can we go out on deck? Possiamo andare sul ponte?
pos-yahmo an-dahray sool pohntay

What is the sea like today? Com'è il mare oggi?
kohme eel mahray od-jee

captain	il capitano
	kapee-tahno
crew	un equipaggio
	aykwee-pad-jo
hovercraft	l'hovercraft
	hovercraft
life jacket	il salvagente
	salva-jayntay
lifeboat	la scialuppa di salvateggio
	shaloop-pa dee salva-tayd-jo
purser	il commissario di bordo
	komees-sahr-yo dee bordo
rough	mosso
	mos-so
ship	la nave
	navay
smooth	calmo
	kalmo
the Channel	la Manica
	manee-ka

beef
il manzo
mandzo

bread
il pane
pahnay

butter
il burro
boor-ro

cheese
il formaggio
formad-jo

chicken
il pollo
pohl-lo

coffee
il caffè
kaf-fe

cream
la panna
pan-na

eggs
le uova
wova

fish
il pesce
payshay

flour
la farina
fa-reena

ham
il prosciutto
proshoot-to

jam
la marmellata
mahrmayl-lahta

kidneys
i rognoni
rohn-yohnee

kilo
il chilo
keelo

lamb
l'agnello
an-yel-lo

litre
il litro
leetro

liver
il fegato
fay-gato

margarine
la margarina
mahrga-reena

milk
il latte
lat-tay

mince
la carne macinata
kahrnay machee-nahta

mustard
il senape
se-napay

oil
l'olio
ol-yoh

pepper
il pepe
paypay

pork
il maiale
ma-yahlay

pound
mezzo chilo
medz-zo keelo

rice
il riso
reezo

salt
il sale
sahlay

soup
la minestra
mee-nestra

steak
la bistecca
beestayk-ka

sugar
lo zucchero
tsook-kayro

tea
il tè
te

tin
la scatola
skah-tola

veal
il vitello
veetayl-lo

vinegar
l'aceto
a-chayto

yoghurt
lo yogurt
yogurt

apples
le mele
maylay

asparagus
gli asparagi
aspa-rajee

aubergine
la melanzana
maylant-sahna

avocado
un avocado
avo-kahdo

bananas
le banane
ba-nanay

beetroot
la barbabietola
bahrbab-ye-tola

carrots
le carote
ka-rotay

cauliflower
il cavolfiore
kahvolf-yohray

celery
il sedano
se-dano

cherries
le ciliegie
cheel-ye-jay

courgettes
gli zucchini
tsook-keenee

cucumber
il cetriolo
chaytree-olo

french beans
i fagiolini
fahjo-leenee

garlic
un aglio
al-yo

grapefruit
il pompelmo
pom-paylmo

grapes
l'uva
oova

leeks
i porri
por-ree

lemon
il limone
lee-mohnay

lettuce
la lattuga
lat-tooga

melon
il melone
may-lohnay

mushrooms
i funghi
foongee

olives
le olive
o-leevay

onions
le cipolle
cheepohl-lay

oranges
le arancie
a-ranchay

peaches
le pesche
peskay

pears
le pere
payray

peas
i piselli
peezel-lee

pepper
il peperone
paypay-rohnay

pineapple
un ananas
a-nanas

plums
le susine
soo-seenay

potatoes
le patate
pa-tahtay

radishes
i ravanelli
rava-nel-lee

raspberries
i lamponi
lam-pohnee

spinach
gli spinaci
spee-nachee

strawberries
le fragole
frah-golay

tomatoes
i pomodori
pohmoh-doree

Where can we buy souvenirs of the cathedral? Dove si possono comprare souvenir sul duomo?
dohvay see pos-sono kom-prahray soov-neer sool dwomo

Where is the nearest gift shop? Dov'è il negozio di articoli da regalo più vicino?
dohve eel naygots-yo dee ahrtee-kolee da ray-gahlo pee-oo vee-cheeno

I want to buy a present for my husband/wife Voglio comprare un regalo per mio marito/mia moglie
vol-yo kom-prahray oon ray-gahlo payr mee-oo ma-reeto/mee-a mol-yay

What is the local/regional speciality? Quali sono le specialità locali/regionali?
kwahlee sohnoh lay spaycha-leeta lo-kahlee/rayjo-nahlee

Is this hand-made? È fatto a mano?
e fahto a mahno

Have you anything suitable for a young child? Avete qualcosa che vada bene per un bambino piccolo?
a-vaytay kwal-koza kay vahda benay payr oon bam-beeno peek-kolo

I want something cheaper/more expensive Voglio qualcosa (di) più economico/costoso
vol-yo kwal-koza (dee) pee-oo ayko-no-meeko/kohs-tohzoh

Will this cheese/wine travel well? Questo formaggio/vino si conserverà bene in viaggio?
kwaysto formad-jo/veeno see konsayr-vayra benay een vee-ad-jo

bracelet
il braccialetto
brat-chalayt-to

brooch
la spilla
speel-la

chocolates
i cioccolatini
chok-kola-teenee

earrings
gli orecchini
orayk-keenee

flowers
i fiori
fee-o-ree

necklace
una collana
kol-lahna

ornament
un ornamento
orna-maynto

perfume
il profumo
pro-foomo

pottery
la terracotta
tayr-ra-kot-ta

ring
un anello
a-nel-lo

table linen
la tovaglia
toval-ya

watch
un orologio
ohroh-lojo

Nouns

In Italian, all nouns are either *masculine* or *feminine*. Where in English we say 'the apple' and 'the book', in Italian it is *la mela* and *il libro* because *mela* is feminine and *libro* is masculine.
The gender of nouns is shown in the 'article' (= words for 'the' and 'a') used before them:

WORDS FOR 'THE'
masc. sing. **il, l'** (+*vowel*)   *fem. sing.* **la, l'** (+*vowel*)
           lo (+*z, gn, pn, ps, x,*
                s+consonant)
masc. plur. **i, gli** (+*vowel,* +*z,*   *fem. plur.* **le**
           gn, pn etc)

WORDS FOR 'A'
masculine   **un, uno** (+*z, gn, pn etc*)
feminine   **una, un'** (+*vowel*)
NOTE: When used after the words **a** (*to, at*), **da** (*by, from*), **su** (*on*), **di** (*of*) and **in** (*in, into*), the words for 'the' contract as follows:

a+il → al	da+il → dal	su+il → sul
a+lo → allo	da+lo → dallo	su+lo → sullo
a+l' → all'	da+l' → dall'	su+l' → sull'
a+la → alla	da+la → dalla	su+la → sulla
a+i → ai	da+i → dai	su+i → sui
a+gli → agli	da+gli → dagli	su+gli → sugli
a+le → alle	da+le → dalle	su+le → sulle

di+il → del	in+il → nel
di+lo → dello	in+lo → nello
di+l' → dell'	in+l' → nell'
di+la → della	in+la → nella
di+i → dei	in+i → nei
di+gli → degli	in+gli → negli
di+le → delle	in+le → nelle

e.g. **alla casa** (to the house)
    sul tavolo (on the table)

Nouns: formation of plurals

For most nouns, the singular ending changes as follows:

masc. sing.	masc. plur.	example
-o	-i	libro → libri
-e	-i	padre → padri
-a	-i	artista → artisti

NOTE: Most nouns ending in **-co/-go** become **-chi/-ghi** in the plural; nouns ending in **-ca/-ga** become **-chi/-ghi.**

fem. sing.	fem. plur.	example
-a	-e	mela → mele
-e	-i	madre → madri

NOTE: Nouns ending in **-ca/-ga** become **-che/-ghe** in the plural; **-cia/-gia** often becomes **-ce/-ge.**

Adjectives

Adjectives normally *follow* the noun they describe in Italian, e.g. la mela **rossa** (*the red apple*).
Some common exceptions which *precede* the noun are:
bello *beautiful*, **breve** *short*, **brutto** *ugly*, **buono** *good*, **cattivo** *bad*, **giovane** *young*, **grande** *big*, **lungo** *long*, **nuovo** *new*, **piccolo** *small*, **vecchio** *old*.
Italian adjectives have to reflect the gender of the noun they describe. To make an adjective **feminine**, an **-a** replaces the **-o** of the masculine, e.g. **rosso** → **rossa**. Adjectives ending in **-e** e.g. **giovane,** can be either masculine or feminine. The plural forms of the adjective change in the way described for nouns (above).

'My', 'Your', 'His', 'Her'

These words also depend on the gender and number of the following noun and *not* on the sex of the 'owner':

	with masc. sing. noun	with fem. sing. noun	with masc. plur. noun	with fem. plur. noun
my	il mio	la mia	i miei	le mie
your (: *polite*)	il suo	la sua	i suoi	le sue
(: *plural*)	il vostro	la vostra	i vostri	le vostre
his/her	il suo	la sua	i suoi	le sue

Pronouns

SUBJECT		OBJECT	
I	io	me	mi
you	lei	you	la
he	lui, egli	him	lo, l' (+*vowel*)
she	lei, ella	her	la, l' (+*vowel*)
it (*masc.*)	esso	it (*masc.*)	lo, l'
(*fem.*)	essa	(*fem.*)	la, l'
we	noi	us	ci
you	voi	you	vi
they	loro	them (*masc.*)	li
(*things: masc.*)	essi	(*fem.*)	le
(*: fem.*)	esse		

NOTES:

1. The subject pronouns are often omitted before Italian verbs, since the verb ending generally distinguishes the person:
   vado ...
   I am going ...

2. **Lei** is the polite form for 'you'; **voi** is the plural form.

3. The object pronouns shown above are used to mean *to me, to us* etc, except:
   to him/it = **gli**
   to her/it; to you = **le**
   to them = **loro**

4. Pronoun objects (other than **loro**) usually *precede* the verb:
   lo vedo   BUT: scriverò **loro**
   I see him   I will write to them

   Used with an infinitive (=the verb form given in the dictionary), however, the pronoun *follows* and is attached to the infinitive minus its final '**e**':
   voglio compra**rlo**
   I want to buy it

Verbs

There are three main patterns of endings for verbs in Italian -
those ending **-are**, **-ere** and **-ire** in the dictionary. Two
examples of the **-ire** verbs are shown, since two distinct groups
of endings exist. Subject pronouns are shown in brackets
because these are often not used (see p. 47):

	parlare	to speak	**vendere**	to sell
(io)	**parlo**	I speak	**vendo**	I sell
(lei)	**parla**	you speak	**vende**	you sell
(lui/lei)	**parla**	he/she speaks	**vende**	he/she sells
(noi)	**parliamo**	we speak	**vendiamo**	we sell
(voi)	**parlate**	you speak	**vendete**	you sell
(loro)	**parlano**	they speak	**vendono**	they sell

	dormire	to sleep	**finire**	to finish
(io)	**dormo**	I sleep	**finisco**	I finish
(lei)	**dormi**	you sleep	**finisci**	you finish
(lui/lei)	**dorme**	he/she sleeps	**finisce**	he/she finishes
(noi)	**dormiamo**	we sleep	**finiamo**	we finish
(voi)	**dormite**	you sleep	**finite**	you finish
(loro)	**dormono**	they sleep	**finiscono**	they finish

And in the past:

	ho parlato	I spoke	**ho venduto**	I sold
(io)	**ho parlato**	I spoke	**ho venduto**	I sold
(lei)	**ha parlato**	you spoke	**ha venduto**	you sold
(lui/lei)	**ha parlato**	he/she spoke	**ha venduto**	she sold
(noi)	**abbiamo parlato**	we spoke	**abbiamo venduto**	we sold
(voi)	**avete parlato**	you spoke	**avete venduto**	you sold
(loro)	**hanno parlato**	they spoke	**hanno venduto**	they sold

	ho dormito	I slept	**ho finito**	I finished
(io)	**ho dormito**	I slept	**ho finito**	I finished
(lei)	**ha dormito**	you slept	**ha finito**	you finished
(lui/lei)	**ha dormito**	she slept	**ha finito**	he/she finished
(noi)	**abbiamo dormito**	we slept	**abbiamo finito**	we finished
(voi)	**avete dormito**	you slept	**avete finito**	you finished
(loro)	**hanno dormito**	they slept	**hanno finito**	they finished

See also GRAMMAR.
Remember that familiar forms are only used when you know
someone well or are invited to do so. Otherwise use the formal
forms. Similarly, 'Ciao' (hello) is only used to greet people you
are on familiar terms with. The words 'Signore', 'Signora', and
'Signorina' are used far more frequently than 'Sir' or 'Madam'
are used in English. Thus, in hotels you are likely to be greeted
with 'Buon giorno Signore' etc. Likewise, you should say 'Buona
sera, Signore' to an official rather than simply 'Buona sera'.

Hello Buon giorno
bwon jorno

Good morning/Good afternoon/Good evening Buon
giorno/Buona sera/Buona sera
bwon jorno/bwona sayra/bwona sayra

Goodbye Arrivederci
ar-reevay-dayrchee

Good night Buona notte
bwona not-tay

How do you do? Piacere!
pee-a-chayray

Pleased to meet you Piacere di conoscerla
pee-a-chayray dee ko-no-shayrla

How nice to see you Che piacere incontrarla
kay pee-a-chayray eenkon-trahrla

How are you? Come sta?
kohmay sta

Fine thank you Bene grazie
Benay grats-yay

See you soon A presto
a presto

See you later A più tardi
a pee-oo tahrdee

I'd like to make an appointment Vorrei prendere un appuntamento
*vor-**re**-ee **pren**-dayray oon ap-**poonta**-maynto*

A cut and blow-dry please Vorrei tagliare i capelli e fare la messa in piega con il föhn
*vor-**re**-ee tal-**yah**ray ee ka**payl**-lee ay fahray la mays-sa een pee-e-ga kohn eel fon*

A shampoo and set Vorrei fare la messa in piega
*vor-**re**-ee fahray la mays-sa een pee-e-ga*

Not too short Non troppo corti
nohn trop-po kortee

I'd like it layered Mi piacciono scalati
*mee pee-**at**-chono ska-**lahtee***

Not too much off the back/the fringe Non tagli troppo dietro/la frangia
*nohn tal-yee trop-poh dee-**e**-tro/la franja*

Take more off the top/the sides Tagli di più sopra/ai lati
talyee dee pee-oo sohpra/a-ee lahtee

My hair is permed/tinted I miei capelli hanno la permanente/sono tinti
*ee mee-**e**-ee ka-**payl**-lee an-no la payrma-**nentay**/sohnoh teentee*

My hair is naturally curly/straight I miei capelli sono mossi/dritti al naturale
*ee mee-**e**-ee ka-**payl**-lee sohnoh mos-see/dreet-tee al natoo-**rahlay***

It's too hot È troppo caldo
e trop-poh kaldo

I'd like a conditioner please Vorrei un balsamo per favore
*vor-**re**-ee oon **bal**-samo payr fa-**vohray***

---

gown
la mantellina
*mantayl-**leena***

hair cut
il taglio
tal-yo

hair spray
la lacca
lak-ka

long
lunghi
loongee

parting
la riga
reega

perm
la permanente
*payrma-**nentay***

shampoo
lo shampoo
shampoo

short
corto
korto

streaks
mèches
mesh

styling mousse
il fissatore
*fees-sa-**tohray***

towel
un asciugamano
*ashoo-ga-**mahno***

trim
la spuntata
*spoon-**tahta***

See also ACCOMMODATION, ROOM SERVICE, PAYING.

I have reserved a room in the name of ... Ho prenotato una stanza a nome di ...
*o prayno-**tahto** oona stantsa a nohmay dee ...*

I confirmed my booking by phone/by letter Ho confermato la prenotazione con una telefonata/lettera
*o konfayr-**mahto** la prayno-tats-**yohnay** kohn oona taylay-fo-**nahta**/**let**-tayra*

What time is breakfast/dinner? A che ora è la colazione/la cena?
*a kay ohra e la kolats-**yohnay**/la chayna*

Can we have breakfast in our room at ... o'clock? Ci può portare la colazione nella nostra stanza alle ...?
*chee pwo por-**tahray** la kolats-**yohnay** nel-la nostra stantsa al-lay ...*

Please call me at seven thirty Per favore chiamatemi alle sette e mezza
*payr fa-**vohray** kee-a-**mah**-taymee al-lay set-tay ay medz-za*

Can I have my key? Posso avere la mia chiave?
*pos-so a-**vayray** la mee-a kee-**ahvay***

Do you have any messages for me? Avete qualche messaggio per me?
*a-**vaytay** kwalkay mays**sad**-jo payr may*

Can we have a packed lunch for our picnic? Potremmo avere un cestino con il pranzo per il picnic?
*po**traym**-mo a-**vayray** oon chay-**steeno** kohn eel prantso payr eel peekneek*

I shall be leaving at 8 o'clock tomorrow morning Partirò domani mattina alle 8
*pahrtee-**ro** do-**mahnee** mat-**teena** al-lay ot-to*

bar il bar *bar*	
desk la ricezione *reechayts-**yohnay***	
lift un ascensore *ashayn-**sohray***	
lounge la sala *sahla*	
manager il direttore *deerayt-**tohray***	
porter il portiere *port-**ye**-ray*	
reservation la prenotazione *prayno-tats-**yohnay***	
restaurant il ristorante *reesto-**rantay***	
room service il servizio da camera *sayr**veets**-yo da ka-mayra*	
stay la permanenza *payrma-**nentsa***	
TV lounge la sala TV *sahla teevoo*	

Where do I check in my luggage? Dove posso consegnare i bagagli?
dohvay pos-so konsayn-yahray ee bagal-yee

Where is the luggage from the London flight/train? Dove sono i bagagli del volo/treno da Londra?
dohvay sohnoh ee bagal-yee dayl vohloh/treno da lohndra

Our luggage has not arrived I nostri bagagli non sono arrivati
ee nostree ba-gal-yee nohn sohnoh ar-ree-vahtee

My suitcase was damaged in transit La mia valigia è stata danneggiata durante il viaggio
la mee-a va-leeja e stahta dan-nayd-jahta doo-rantay eel vee-ad-jo

Where is the left-luggage office? Dov'è il deposito bagagli?
dohve eel daypo-zeeto bagal-yee

Are there any luggage trolleys? Ci sono dei carrelli per i bagagli?
chee sohnoh day-ee kar-rel-lee payr ee bagal-yee

My case is very heavy La mia valigia è molto pesante
la mee-a va-leeja e mohltoh pay-santay

Can you help me with my bags please? Può aiutarmi a portare le valigie per favore?
pwo a-yoo-tahrmee a por-tahray lay va-leejay payr fa-vohray

Please take my bags to a taxi Per favore porti le mie valigie al taxi
payr fa-vohray portee lay mee-ay va-leejay al taxee

baggage reclaim	il ritiro bagagli *ree-teero bagal-yee*
excess luggage	il bagaglio in eccedenza *bagal-yo een aytchay-dentsa*
flight bag	la borsa da viaggio *borsa da vee-ad-jo*
hand luggage	il bagaglio a mano *bagal-yo a mahno*
locker	un armadietto *ahrmad-yayt-to*
luggage allowance	il bagaglio permesso *bagal-yo payrmays-so*
luggage rack	il portabagagli *porta-bagal-yee*
porter	il facchino *fak-keeno*
trunk	il baule *ba-oolay*

See also DIRECTIONS.

Where can I buy a local map? Dove posso comprare una cartina?
dohvay pos-so kom-prahray oona kahr-teena

Have you got a town plan? Avete una piantina della città?
a-vaytay oona pee-an-teena dayl-la cheet-ta

I want a street map of the city Voglio una piantina della città
vol-yo oona pee-an-teena dayl-la cheet-ta

I need a road map of ... Ho bisogno di una carta stradale di ...
o beezohn-yo dee oona kahrta stra-dahlay dee ...

Can I get a map at the tourist office? Posso prendere una cartina all'ufficio informazioni turistiche?
pos-so pren-dayray oona kahr-teena al-loo-feecho eenfor-mats-yohnee tooree-steekay

Can you show me on the map? Può mostrarmelo sulla cartina?
pwo mostrahr-melo sool-la kahr-teena

Do you have a guidebook in English? Avete una guida in inglese?
a-vaytay oona gweeda een een-glayzay

Do you have a guidebook to the cathedral? Avete una guida sulla cattedrale?
a-vaytay oona gweeda sool-la kat-taydrahlay

I need an English-Italian dictionary Ho bisogno di un dizionario inglese-italiano
o beezohn-yo dee oon deets-yo-nar-yo een-glayzay eetal-yahno

Do you have an English phrasebook? Avete un vocabolarietto di inglese?
a-vaytay oon voka-bolahr-yayt-to dee een-glayzay

See also BUYING, CONVERSION CHARTS, NUMBERS, PAYING

a pint of ...
un mezzo litro di ...
oon medz-zo leetro dee

a third
un terzo
oon tertso

a litre of ...
un litro di ...
oon leetro dee

two thirds
due terzi
doo-ay tertsee

a kilo of ...
un kilo di ...
oon keelo dee

a quarter
un quarto
oon kwarto

a pound of ...
un mezzo kilo di...
oon medz-zo keelo dee

three quarters
tre quarti
tray kwartee

100 grammes of ...
un etto di...
oon et-to dee

ten per cent
il dieci per cento
eel dee-e-chee payr chento

half a kilo of ...
un mezzo kilo di ...
oon medz-zo keelo dee

more of
più di
pee-oo dee

a half-bottle of ...
un mezzo litro di...
oon medz-zo leetro dee

less of
meno di
mayno dee

a slice of ...
una fetta di...
oona fayt-ta dee

enough of
abbastanza
ab-ba-stantsa

a portion of ...
una porzione di ...
oona portsee-oh-nay dee

double
il doppio
eel dop-pee-o

a dozen ...
una dozzina di ...
oona dodz-zeena dee

twice
due volte
dooay voltay

1500 lira's worth ...
1500 lire di ...
meel-lay-cheen-kway-chento leeray dee

three times
tre volte
tray voltay

See also EATING OUT, FOOD, WINES AND SPIRITS, WINE LIST

Starters - Antipasti

Antipasto misto Mixed hors d'oeuvres
Asparagi Asparagus
Crostini di fegatini Fried bread with chicken livers
Prosciutto e fichi Parma ham with fresh figs
Salmone affumicato Smoked salmon

Fish Dishes - Pesce

Acciughe ripiene Fresh anchovies stuffed with cheese, fried
Anguille in carpione Fried eels
Aragosta Lobster
Baccalà alla vicentina Salt cod cooked in milk with spices
Calamari in umido Squid in oil
Cozze fritte Mussels in batter, fried
Cozze gratinate Mussels in half a shell covered in parsley, garlic and breadcrumbs and browned in the oven
Fritto misto di mare Mixed fried shellfish
Gamberoni alla griglia Charcoal-grilled large prawns
Muggine Rock mullet
Ostriche Oysters, fried in breadcrumbs
Sa cassola Sardinian fish stew
Sarde Fresh sardines cooked in olive oil and oregano
Sogliola alla griglia Grilled sole
Sogliola alla mugnaia Sole in a white wine sauce
Trota ai ferri Grilled trout
Trota alla valdostana Poached trout in a butter sauce

Soups and Pasta - Minestre e Farinacei

Brodetto di pesce Spicy fish soup
Calzone A type of pizza
Cannelloni Rolls of pasta stuffed with various fillings
Fettuccine Long flat strips of pasta
Gnocchi alla fontina Dumplings with melted cheese
Gnocchi al pesto Small potato dumplings with a sauce of basil, garlic, pine nuts and pecorino cheese
Lasagne al forno Layers of pasta and (meat) sauce with a cheese/bechamel topping, oven-baked
Lasagne verdi Layers of spinach (green) pasta
Minestrone Thick vegetable soup
Minestrone alla genovese Vegetable soup flavoured with a cheese and herb mixture (pesto)
Paglia e fieno White and green pasta cooked in different ways
Panzerotti Pasta cushions filled with cheese and ham, fried
Pasticcio A sort of pasta pie
Penne Quill-shaped tubes of pasta
Pizza ai funghi Pizza with garlic, mushrooms, parsley and olive oil
Pizza napoletana Pizza with tomatoes, mozzarella cheese, basil, olive oil and parmesan cheese
Ravioli di spinaci Square pasta cushions filled with spinach and parmesan cheese
Risotto alla milanese Rice dish with mushrooms and cheese
Spaghetti alla carbonara Spaghetti with chopped bacon and a sauce of egg yolks, cream and black pepper
Spaghetti alle vongole Spaghetti with a clam sauce
Stracciatella Clear soup with eggs and cheese stirred in
Tagliatelle Ribbon-like pasta
Tortellini in brodo Small stuffed coils of pasta in broth
Tortellini alla bolognese Small stuffed coils of pasta with a cheese and butter topping
Trenette al pesto Variety of tagliatelle with a sauce of basil, garlic, pine nuts and pecorino cheese
Vermicelli Thin strings of pasta
Zuppa di cipolle Onion soup
Zuppa di datteri Shellfish soup
Zuppa di pesce Fish soup

Meat Dishes - Carne

Agnello arrosto Roast lamb
Bistecca ai ferri Grilled steak
Bistecca alla pizzaiola Steak with a tomato and herb sauce
Bocconcini Rolls of veal with ham and cheese filling
Carpaccio Sliced raw lean beef with lemon juice
Cima alla genovese Veal stuffed with minced meat, eggs, vegetables and pistachio nuts, served cold
Cinghiale alla cacciatora Wild boar braised in white wine
Coniglio alla cacciatora Rabbit cooked in white wine
Costoletta alla bolognese Veal cutlet with ham and cheese
Cotechino A type of salami served hot in slices
Fegato alla veneziana Calves' liver and onions
Fiorentina Grilled T-bone steak
Frittata di prosciutto Ham omelette
Fritto misto Fried meats and vegetables; sort of mixed grill
Involtini Rolls of veal with ham or chicken filling
Lepre in agrodolce Hare in a sweet and sour sauce
Maiale arrosto Roast pork
Osso Buco Shin of veal cooked in wine with tomatoes
Piccata al limone Veal cutlets cooked in butter, lemon juice
Porchetta Roast sucking pig
Prosciutto crudo/di Parma Raw/Parma ham
Saltimbocca Veal escalopes with ham and sage
Scaloppa milanese Veal escalope fried in breadcrumbs
Strecchini alla bolognese Chicken livers, sweetbreads, etc skewered with cheese, oven-baked in a white sauce
Stufato di manzo Beef stewed with tomatoes, onions, sage
Trippa alla parmigiana Tripe with butter and parmesan
Vitello bolognese Veal escalopes with Parma ham, parmesan
Vitello tonnato Veal in tuna fish sauce, served cold
Zampone Pig's trotter stuffed with minced pork and spices

Poultry - Pollame

Anitra in agrodolce Duck in sweet and sour sauce
Fagiano Pheasant
Petto di pollo Breast of chicken
Pollo alla diavola Charcoal-grilled chicken with lemon juice
Tacchino in gelatina Turkey in aspic served in slices

Vegetables - Contorni

Caponata Aubergines, onions, celery, peppers, tomatoes, olives, courgettes, pine nuts, garlic and herbs
Carciofi alla romana Stuffed artichokes, sautéed
Fagioli toscani con tonno White beans, tuna fish in oil
Insalata mista Mixed salad
Insalata di pomodori Tomato salad
Melanzane alla parmigiana Aubergines cooked with layers of ham, tomato or meat sauce topped with parmesan
Melanzane ripiene Stuffed aubergines
Patate fritte Fried potatoes
Peperonata Sliced peppers cooked in a rich tomato sauce with onions and spices
Piselli e prosciutto Peas with ham, onions and bacon
Polenta Yellow maize flour served in many different ways; often plain with sausages or baked with sauces
Pomodori ripieni Stuffed tomatoes
Puré di patate Mashed potatoes
Zucchini fritti Sliced courgettes fried in batter

Cheese - Formaggi

Bel Paese Soft, mild creamy cheese
Dolcelatte Mild, creamy blue cheese
Gorgonzola Soft, sharp blue cheese
Mascarpone Mild, creamy cheese often served as a dessert
Mozzarella Soft, mild white cheese; often used in pizza
Parmigiano Parmesan; Hard cheese usually grated in recipes, but also eaten fresh
Pecorino Hard, sharp-tasting ewe's milk cheese
Ricotta Creamy curd cheese; often served as a dessert

Desserts - Dolci

Castagnaccio Chestnut cake with pine nuts and sultanas
Cassata Ice cream with candied fruit
Gelato Ice cream
Gianduia Cold chocolate pudding
Granita Water Ice
Macedonia Fresh fruit salad
Panettone Christmas cake; sultana bread
Pesche al vino Sliced fresh peaches in white or red wine
Ricciarelli Almond biscuits
Semifreddo Ice cream cake
Sfogliatelle Flaky pastry with cream cheese and fruit
Zabaglione Whipped egg yolks and sugar with marsala wine
Zuppa inglese A sort of trifle

Understanding the Menu

al forno oven-baked
al gratin oven-baked with breadcrumb topping
all'aglio with garlic
alla griglia grilled
alla panna with cream
allo spiedo spit-roasted
bollito boiled
col vino (bianco/rosso) with (white/red) wine
con contorno with vegetables
condimento per insalata vinaigrette
impanato e fritto fried in breadcrumbs
farcito with garnish/stuffed
fritto fried
in agrodolce sweet and sour
lesso boiled
misto mixed
ripieno stuffed

I haven't enough money Non ho abbastanza soldi
*nohn o ab-ba-**stant**sta soldee*

Have you any change? Avete da cambiare?
*a-**vay**tay da kamb-**yah**ray*

Can you change a 50,000 lire note? Può cambiare un biglietto da 50.000 lire?
*pwo kamb-**yah**ray oon beel-**yayt**-to da cheenkwan-ta-**mee**la leeray*

I'd like to change these traveller's cheques Vorrei cambiare questi traveller's cheque
*vor-**re**-ee kamb-**yah**ray kwaystee travellers cheque*

I want to change some lire into pounds Vorrei cambiare queste lire in sterline
*vor-**re**-ee kamb-**yah**ray kwaystay leeray een stayr-**lee**nay*

What is the rate for sterling? Qual'è il cambio per la sterlina?
*kwah**le** eel kamb-yo payr la stayr-**lee**na*

Can I get a cash advance with my credit card? Posso avere un anticipo con la mia carta di credito?
*pos-so a-**vay**ray oon antee-cheepo kohn la mee-a karta dee **kray**-deeto*

I should like to transfer some money from my account in ... Vorrei trasferire alcuni soldi dal mio conto a ...
*vor-**re**-ee trasfay-**ree**ray al-**koo**nee soldee dal mee-o kohntoh a ...*

How do I get reimbursed? Come si fa per essere rimborsati?
*kohmay see fa payr es-sayray reembor-**sah**tee*

bank
la banca
banka

bureau de change
un ufficio di cambio
*oof-**fee**cho dee kamb-yo*

cash
contanti
*kon-**tan**tee*

cheque book
il libretto degli assegni
*leebrayt-to dayl-lyee as-**sayn**-yee*

currency
la valuta
*va-**loo**ta*

exchange rate
il cambio
kamb-yo

notes
le banconote
*bankoh-**no**tay*

post office
un ufficio postale
*oof-**fee**cho po-**stah**lay*

purse
il borsellino
*borsayl-**lee**no*

wallet
il portafoglio
*porta-**fol**-yo*

See also EATING OUT, ENTERTAINMENT.

What is there to do in the evenings? Che cosa si può fare di sera?
kay koza see pwo fahray dee sayra

Where can we go to see a cabaret/go to dance? Dove possiamo andare per vedere un cabaret/per ballare?
dohvay pos-yahmo an-dahray payr vay-dayray oon kaba-re/payr bal-lahray

Are there any good night clubs/discos? Ci sono dei buoni locali notturni/delle buone discoteche?
chee sohnoh day-ee bwonee lo-kahlee not-toornee/dayl-lay bwonay deesko-tekay

How do we get to the casino? Come ci si arriva al casinò?
kohmay chee see ar-reeva al kazee-no

Do we need to be members? Bisogna essere soci?
beezohn-ya es-sayray sochee

How much does it cost to get in? Quanto costa il biglietto di entrata?
kwanto kohsta eel beel-yayt-to dee ayn-trahta

We'd like to reserve two seats for tonight Vorremmo prenotare due posti per stasera
vor-raym-mo prayno-tahray doo-ay pohstee payr sta-sayra

Is there a bar/a restaurant? C'è un bar/un ristorante?
che oon bar/oon reesto-rantay

What time does the show/concert begin? A che ora inizia lo spettacolo/il concerto?
a kay ohra eeneets-ya loh spayt-tah-kolo/eel kon-chayrto

How long does the performance last? Quanto dura lo spettacolo?
kwanto doora loh spayt-tah-kolo

Which film is on at the cinema? Che film c'è al cinema?
kay feelm che al chee-nayma

Can we get there by bus/taxi? Possiamo andarci con l'autobus/il taxi?
pos-yahmo an-dahrchee kohn low-toboos/eel taxee

See also ROAD SIGNS

Acqua potabile
Drinking water

Affittasi
For hire, To rent

Ai treni
To the trains

ALT
Stop

Aperto
Open

Ascensore
Lift

Biglietti
Tickets

Caldo
Hot

Camere
Rooms to let

Cassa
Cash desk

Chiuso
Closed

Completo
No vacancies

**Convalidare il
  biglietto qui**
Please punch your
  ticket here

Deposito bagagli
Left luggage

Divieto di balneazione
No bathing

Enoteca
Wine tasting

Entrata
Entrance

Entrata libera
Free admission

Freddo
Cold

Fumatori
Smokers, Smoking

Fuori servizio
Out of order

Informazioni
Information, Enquiries

Libero
Free, Vacant

Non fumatori
Non-smokers,
  No smoking

Occupato
Engaged

Pianoterra
Ground Floor

Privato
Private

Proprietà privata
Private property

Saldi
Sale

Self-service
Self-service

Seminterrato
Basement

Signore
Ladies

Signori
Gentlemen, Men

Spingere
Push

Spuntini
Snacks

Suonare
Ring

Tintoria
Dry Cleaner's

Tirare
Pull

**Ufficio informazioni
  turistiche**
Tourist Information
  Office

Uscita
Exit

Uscita d'emergenza
Emergency exit

Vendesi
For Sale

**Vietato calpestare
  l'erba**
Do not walk on the
  grass

Vietato fumare
No smoking

Vietato l'ingresso
Keep out, No entry

See also MEASUREMENTS AND QUANTITIES

0	zero *dzero*	13	tredici *tray-deechee*	50	cinquanta *cheenkwan-ta*
1	uno, una *oono, oona*	14	quattordici *kwat-tor-deechee*	60	sessanta *says-santa*
2	due *dooay*	15	quindici *kween-deechee*	70	settanta *sayt-tanta*
3	tre *tray*	16	sedici *say-deechee*	80	ottanta *oht-tanta*
4	quattro *kwat-tro*	17	diciasette *deechas-set-tay*	90	novanta *noh-vanta*
5	cinque *cheen-kway*	18	diciotto *deechot-to*	100	cento *chento*
6	sei *se-ee*	19	diciannove *deechan-novay*	110	cento dieci *chento-dee-e-chee*
7	sette *set-te*	20	venti *vayntee*	200	duecento *doo-ay-chento*
8	otto *ot-to*	21	ventuno *vayn-toono*	300	trecento *tray-chento*
9	nove *novay*	22	ventidue *vayntee-doo-ay*	1,000	mille *meel-lay*
10	dieci *dee-e-chee*	23	ventitre *vayntee-tray*	2,000	duemila *doo-ay-meela*
11	undici *oon-deechee*	30	trenta *trayn-ta*	1,000,000	un milione *oon meel-yohnay*
12	dodici *doh-deechee*	40	quaranta *kwaran-ta*		

1st	primo *preemo*		6th	sesto *sesto*	
2nd	secondo *saykohn-do*		7th	settimo *set-teemo*	
3rd	terzo *tayrtso*		8th	ottavo *oht-tahvo*	
4th	quarto *kwarto*		9th	nono *nonoh*	
5th	quinto *kweento*		10th	decimo *dechee-mo*	

See also COMPLAINTS, EATING OUT, MENUS, WINES AND
SPIRITS.

**Do you have a set menu/a special
menu for children?** Avete un menu
fisso/un menu speciale per bambini?
*a-vaytay oon maynoo fees-so/oon maynoo
spay-chahlay payr bam-beenee*

We will have the menu at 10,000 lire
Prendiamo il menu a 10.000 lire
*prend-yahmo eel maynoo a dee-etchee-
meela leeray*

May we see the wine list? Possiamo
vedere la lista dei vini?
*pos-yahmo vay-dayray la leesta day-ee
veenee*

What do you recommend? Che cosa ci
consiglia?
kay koza chee konseel-ya

Is there a local speciality? C'è una
specialità locale?
che oona spaycha-leeta lo-kahlay

How is this dish served? Come viene
servito questo piatto?
*kohmay vee-e-nay sayr-veeto kwaysto pee-
at-to*

Are the vegetables included?
Comprende anche i contorni?
kom-prenday ankay ee kon-tornee

Rare/medium rare/well done, please
Al sangue/poco cotta/cotta bene, per
favore
*al sangwe/poko kot-ta/kot-ta benay payr fa-
vohray*

We'd like a dessert/some coffee please
Vorremmo un dolce/il caffè, per favore
*vor-raym-mo oon dohlchay/eel kaf-fe payr
fa-vohray*

bill
il conto
kohntoh

course
il piatto
pee-at-to

cover charge
il coperto
ko-payrto

meal
il pasto
pasto

order
un'ordinazione
ordee-nats-yohnay

service
il servizio
sayrveets-yo

table
il tavolo
tah-volo

that one
quello là
kwayl-lo la

this one
questo qui
kwaysto kwee

waiter
il cameriere
kamayr-ye-ray

waitress
la cameriera
kamayr-ye-ra

See also BUYING, MONEY.

Can I have the bill, please? Mi può portare il conto, per favore?
*mee pwo por-**tah**ray eel kohntoh payr fa-**voh**ray*

Is service/tax included? Il servizio è compreso/L'IVA è compresa?
*eel sayr**veets**-yo e kom-**prayz**o/leeva e kom-**prayz**a*

What does that come to? Quanto fa in tutto?
kwanto fa een toot-to

How much is it? Quanto costa?
kwanto kohsta

Do I pay in advance? Pago in anticipo?
*pahgo een an**tee**-cheepo*

Do I pay a deposit? Devo pagare un acconto?
*dayvo pa-**gah**ray oon ak-**kohn**toh*

Can I pay by cheque? Posso pagare con un assegno?
*pos-so pa-**gah**ray kohn oon as-**sayn**-yo*

Do you accept traveller's cheques? Accettate i traveller's cheque?
*at-chayt-**tah**tay ee travellers cheque*

I don't have enough in cash Non ne ho abbastanza in contanti
*nohn nay o ab-bas-**tant**sa een kon-**tan**tee*

You've given me the wrong change Ha sbagliato a darmi il resto
*a zbal-**yah**to a dahrmee eel resto*

I'd like a receipt, please Vorrei una ricevuta, per favore
*vor-**re**-ee oona reechay-**voo**ta payr fa-**voh**ray*

cash desk	la cassa *kas-sa*
cashier	il cassiere *kas-ye-ray*
charge	il costo *kostoh*
cheaper	meno costoso *mayno koh-stohzoh*
cheque card	la carta assegni *kahrta as-sayn-yee*
discount	lo sconto *skohntoh*
expensive	costoso *koh-stohzoh*
payment	il pagamento *paga-mayntoh*
reduction	la riduzione *reedoots-yohnay*
signature	la firma *feerma*
till	la cassa *kas-sa*

My name is ... Mi chiamo ...
mee kee-ahmo...

My date of birth is ... Sono nato il ...
sohnoh nahto eel ...

My address is ... Il mio indirizzo è ...
eel mee-o eendee-reets-so e ...

I come from Britain/America Vengo
dalla Gran Bretagna/dall'America
vengo dal-la gran braytan-ya/dal-lamay-reeka

I live in London/Scotland Abito a
Londra/in Scozia
ah-beeto a lohndra/een skots-ya

**My passport/driving licence number
is ...** Il numero del mio passaporto/della
mia patente è ...
*eel noo-mayro dayl mee-o pas-sa-porto/
dayl-la mee-a pa-tentay e ...*

My blood group is ... Il mio gruppo
sanguigno è ...
eel mee-o groop-po sangween-yo e ...

I work in an office/a factory Lavoro in
un ufficio/un'industria
la-vohroh een oon oof-feecho/ooneen-doostree-a

I am a secretary/manager Sono una
segretaria/un direttore
sohnoh oona saygray-tar-ya/oon deerayt-tohray

I'm here on holiday/business Sono qui
in vacanza/per affari
sohnoh kwee een va-kantsa/payr af-fahree

There are four of us altogether Siamo
quattro in tutto
see-ahmo kwat-tro een toot-to

My daughter/son is 6 Mia figlia/mio
figlio ha 6 anni
mee-a feel-ya/mee-o feel-yo a se-ee an-nee

blind
cieco
cheko

daughter
figlia
feel-ya

deaf
sordo
sordo

disabled
handicappato
andee-kap-pahto

English
inglese
een-glayzay

husband
il marito
ma-reeto

Irish
irlandese
eerlan-dayzay

Scottish
scozzese
skots-sayzay

son
il figlio
feel-yo

student
lo studente
stoo-dayntay

Welsh
gallese
gal-layzay

wife
la moglie
mol-yay

See also CAR PARTS, DRIVING ABROAD, PAYING.

20 litres of 2 star 20 litri di normale
vayntee leetree dee nor-mahlay

10,000 liras' (worth) of 4 star 10.000 lire
di super per favore
*dee-e-chee-meela leeray dee soopayr payr
fa-vohray*

Fill it up please Il pieno, per favore
eel pee-e-no payr fa-vohray

Can you check the oil/water? Può
controllare l'olio/l'acqua?
pwo kontrohl-lah-ray lol-yo/lakwa

Top up the windscreen washers Mi può
mettere il liquido per il tergicristallo
*mee pwo mayt-tayray eel lee-kweedo payr
eel tayrgee-kreestal-lo*

Could you clean the windscreen?
Potrebbe pulire il vetro?
potreb-bay poo-leeray eel vaytro

Where's the air line? Dove posso
controllare la pressione delle gomme?
*dohvay pos-so kontrol-lahray la prays-
yohnay dayl-lay gohm-may*

Can I have a can of petrol/oil ? Posso
avere una lattina di benzina/olio
*pos-so a-vayray oona lat-teena dee baynd-
zeena/ol-yo*

Is there a lavatory? C'è un gabinetto?
che oon gabee-nayt-to

How do I use the car wash? Come
funziona il lavaggio auto?
kohmay foonts-yohna eel lavad-jo owto

Can I pay by credit card? Posso pagare
con la carta di credito?
*pos-so pa-gahray kohn la kahrta dee kray-
deeto*

attendant
il benzinaio
bayndzee-na-yo

diesel
il gasolio
gazol-yo

distilled water
l'acqua distillata
akwa deesteel-lahta

garage
un'autorimessa
owto-reemays-sa

hose
il manicotto
manee-cot-toh

petrol pump
il distributore di
benzina
*deestree-boo-
tohray dee baynd-
zeena*

petrol station
la stazione di
servizio
*stats-yohnay dee
sayrveets-yo*

tyre pressure
la pressione delle
gomme
*prays-yohnay dayl-
lay gohm-may*

**windscreen
washers**
il lavacristallo
lahva-kree-stal-lo

I need a colour/black and white film for this camera Ho bisogno di un rullino a colori/in bianco e nero per questa macchina fotografica
o beezohn-yo dee oon rool-leeno a kohlohree/een bee-anko ay nayro payr kwaysta mak-keena foto-gra-feeka

It is for prints/slides È per fotografie/diapositive
e payr foto-gra-fee-ay/dee-a-pozee-teevay

Have you got some flash cubes for this camera? Avete dei flash per questa macchina fotografica?
a-vaytay day-ee flash payr kwaysta mak-keena foto-gra-feeka

The film has jammed Il rullino si è bloccato
eel rool-leeno see e blok-kahto

The rewind mechanism does not work Il meccanismo di ravvolgimento non funziona
eel mayk-ka-neezmo dee rav-voljee-maynto nohn foonts-yohna

Can you develop this film, please? Può sviluppare questo rullino, per favore?
pwo zveeloop-pahray kwaysto rool-leeno payr fa-vohray

When will the photos be ready? Quando saranno pronte le foto?
kwando saran-no prohntay lay fotoh

Can I take photos in here? Posso fare delle foto qui dentro?
pos-so fahray dayl-lay fotoh kwee dayntro

Would you take a photo of us, please? Può farci una foto, per favore?
pwo fahrchee oona fotoh payr fa-vohray

---

cartridge
il caricatore
karee-ka-tohray

cassette
la cassetta
kas-sayt-ta

exposure meter
un esposimetro
ayspo-zee-maytro

flash bulb
la lampadina per il flash
lampa-deena payr eel flash

lens
un obiettivo
ob-yayt-teevo

lens cover
il copri-obiettivo
kopree-ob-yayt-teevo

movie camera
la cinepresa
cheenay-prayza

negative
il negativo
nayga-teevo

reel
il rotolino
roto-leeno

shutter
l'otturatore
ot-toora-tohray

tripod
il treppiede
traypee-e-day

See also ACCIDENTS, CUSTOMS AND PASSPORTS, EMERGENCIES.

We should call the police Dovremmo chiamare la polizia
dovraym-mo kee-a-mahray la poleet-see-a

Where is the police station? Dov'è il posto di polizia?
dohve eel pohstoh dee poleet-see-a

My car has been broken into Mi hanno aperto la macchina
mee an-no a-payrto la mak-keena

I've been robbed Sono stato derubato
sohnoh stahto dayroo-bahto

I have had an accident Ho avuto un incidente
o a-vooto oon eenchee-dentay

How much is the fine? Quant'è la multa?
kwante la moolta

How do I pay it? Come pago?
kohmay pago

Can I pay at a police station? Posso pagare al posto di polizia?
pos-so pa-gahray al pohstoh dee poleet-see-a

I don't have my driving licence on me Non ho la patente con me
nohn o la pa-tentay kohn may

I'm very sorry, officer Mi dispiace molto signor poliziotto
mee deespee-achay mohltoh seen-yohr poleetz-yot-to

I didn't know the regulations Non conoscevo il regolamento
nohn kono-shayvo eel raygo-la-maynto

car number
la targa
tahrga

documents
i documenti
dokoo-mayntee

green card
la carta verde
kahrta vayrday

insurance certificate
il certificato di assicurazione
chayrtee-fee-kahto dee as-seekoo-rats-yohnay

lawyer
un avvocato
av-vo-kahto

police car
la macchina della polizia
mak-keena dayl-la poleet-see-a

policeman
il poliziotto
poleets-yot-to

traffic offence
un'infrazione
eenfrats-yohnay

traffic warden
un addetto al controllo del traffico
ad-dayt-to al kontrol-lo dayl traf-feeko

Stamps can also be bought at a *tabaccheria*. Allow 7 to 10 days for letters to and from Italy.

How much is a letter to England/America? Quanto costa un francobollo per l'Inghilterra/l'America?
*kwanto kohsta oon frankoh-**bohl**loh payr leengeel-**ter**-ra/lamay-**reeka***

I'd like six stamps for postcards to Germany, please Vorrei sei francobolli per cartoline per la Germania, per favore
*vor-**re**-ee se-ee frankoh-**bohl**-lee payr karto-**lee**nay payr la jayr**man**-ya payr fa-**voh**ray*

Twelve 500-lira stamps please Dodici francobolli da 500 lire per favore
***doh**-deechee frankoh-**bohl**-lee da cheenkway-**chayn**to leeray payr fa-**voh**ray*

I want to send a telegram to ... Voglio mandare un telegramma in ...
*vol-yo man-**dah**ray oon taylay-**gram**-ma een ...*

How much will it cost? Quanto potrà costare?
*kwanto potra koh-**stah**ray*

Do I have to fill in a form? C'è bisogno di compilare una scheda?
*che **bee**zohn-yo dee kompee-**lah**ray oona skeda*

I want to send this parcel Voglio spedire questo pacco
*vol-yo spay-**dee**ray kwaysto pak-ko*

I'd like to make a telephone call Vorrei fare una telefonata
*vor-**re**-ee fahray oona taylay-fo-**nata***

air mail
via aerea
*vee-a a-**eray**-a*

clerk
un impiegato
*eemp-ye-**gah**to*

counter
lo sportello
sportel-lo

express (adj)
espresso
*ay**sprays**-so*

international
internazionale
*eentayr-nats-yo-**nah**lay*

money order
il vaglia
val-ya

post office
un ufficio postale
*oof-**feecho** po-**stah**lay*

postage
l'affrancatura (f)
*af-franka-**toora***

registered (adj)
raccomandato
*rak-koman-**dah**to*

reply coupon
la ricevuta di ritorno
*reechay-**voota** dee ree-**torno***

See also ACCIDENTS, COMPLAINTS, EMERGENCIES, POLICE.

Can you help me, please? Può aiutarmi, per favore?
pwo a-yoo-tahrmee payr fa-vohray

What is the matter? Che cosa c'è?
kay koza che

I am in trouble Ho bisogno di aiuto
o beezohn-yo dee a-yooto

I don't understand Non capisco
nohn ka-peesko

Do you speak English? Parla inglese?
parla een-glayzay

Please repeat that Ripeta per favore
ree-pe-ta payr fa-vohray

I have run out of money Sono rimasto senza soldi
schnoh ree-masto sentsa soldee

My son is lost Non trovo più mio figlio
nohn trohvoh pee-oo mee-o feel-yo

I have lost my way Mi sono perso
mee sohnoh payrso

I have forgotten my passport Ho dimenticato il passaporto
o deemayn-tee-kahto eel pas-sa-porto

Please give me my passport back Mi restituisca il passaporto
per favore
mee raystee-too-eeska eel pas-sa-porto payr fa-vohray

Where is the British Consulate? Dov'è il consolato
britannico?
dohve eel konso-lahto breetan-neeko

In the pronunciation system used in this book, Italian sounds are represented by spellings of the nearest possible sounds in English. Hence, when you read out the pronunciation - the line in *italics* after each phrase or word - sound the letters as if you were reading an English word. Whenever we think it is not sufficiently clear where to stress a word or phrase, we have used **heavy italics** to highlight the syllable to be stressed. The following notes should help you:

	REMARKS	EXAMPLE	PRONUNCIATION
ay	As in *day*	**dei**	*day-ee*
ah	As *a* in *father*	**prendiamo**	*prend-yahmo*
e	As in *bed*	**letto**	*let-to*
oh	As in *go, low*	**sono**	*sohnoh*
y	As in *yet*	**aiuto**	*a-yooto*

Spelling in Italian is very regular and, with a little practice, you will soon be able to pronounce Italian words from their spelling alone. The only letters which may cause problems are:

i	As *ee* in *meet*	**vino**	*veeno*
	Or as *y* in *yet*	**aiuto**	*a-yooto*
u	As *oo* in *boot*	**luna**	*loona*
	Or as *w* in *will*	**buon**	*bwon*
c	Before *e, i* as *ch* in *chat*	**centro**	*chentro*
	Before *a, o, u* as in *cat*	**cosa**	*koza*
ch	As *c* in *cat*	**chi**	*kee*
g	Before *e, i* as in *gin*	**giorno**	*jorno*
	Before *a, h, o, u* as in *get*	**regalo**	*ray-gahlo*
gl	As *lli* in *million*	**figlio**	*feel-yo*
gn	As *ni* in *onion*	**bisogno**	*beezohn-yo*
h	Silent	**ho**	*o*
sc	Before *e, i,* as *sh* in *shop*	**uscita**	*oo-sheeta*
	Before *a, o, u* as in *scar*	**capisco**	*ka-peesko*
z	As *ts* in *cats*	**senza**	*sentsa*
	or *ds* in *rods*	**mezzo**	*medz-zo*

New Year's Day	January 1st
Easter Monday	
Liberation Day	April 25th
Labour Day	May 1st
Assumption	August 15th
All Saints' Day	November 1st
Immaculate Conception	December 8th
Christmas Day	December 25th
St Stephen's Day	December 26th

See also LUGGAGE, TRAIN TRAVEL.
Children under ten pay half fare and those under four travel
free. Few trains have snack bars, but at larger stations
refreshments and rolls are sold on the platform.

What time are the trains to ...? A che
ora ci sono i treni per ...?
a kay ohra chee sohnoh ee trenee payr ...

When is the next train to ...? Quando
parte il prossimo treno per ...?
*kwando pahrtay eel pros-seemo treno
payr...*

What time does it get there? A che ora
arriva?
a kay ohra ar-reeva

Do I have to change? Devo cambiare?
dayvo kamb-yahray

A single/return to ..., first/second class
Un biglietto di andata/andata e ritorno per
..., prima/seconda classe
*oonbeel-yayt-to dee an-dahta/an-dahta ay
ree-torno payr ... preema/say-kohnda
klas-say*

**I want to book a seat in a non-smoking
compartment** Voglio prenotare un posto
in uno scompartimento non fumatori
*vol-yo prayno-tahray oon pohstoh een oono
skompar-tee-maynto nohn fooma-tohree*

I want to reserve a couchette/sleeper
Voglio prenotare una cuccetta/un posto sul
vagone letto
*vol-yo prayno-tahray oona koot-chet-ta/
oon pohstoh sool va-gohnay let-to*

Which platform for the train to ...? Da
che binario parte il treno per ...?
Da kay beenar-yo pahrtay eel treno payr ...

arrivals	gli arrivi
	ar-reevee
buffet	il buffet
	boo-fe
departures	le partenze
	par-tentsay
guard	il capotreno
	kapo-trayno
half fare	metà prezzo
	mayta prets-so
left luggage	il deposito bagagli
	daypo-zeeto bagal-yee
reservation	la prenotazione
	prayno-tats-yohnay
ticket office	la biglietteria
	beel-yayt-tayree-a
timetable board	il tabellone degli orari
	tabayl-lohnay dayl-yee o-rahree
waiting room	la sala d'aspetto
	sahla daspet-to

See also ACCIDENTS, BREAKDOWNS, EMERGENCIES.

I have broken the window Ho rotto un vetro
o roht-toh oon vaytro

There is a hole in these trousers C'è un buco in questi pantaloni
che oon booko een kwaystee panta-lohnee

This is broken/torn Questo è rotto/ strappato
kwaysto e roht-toh/strap-pahto

Can you repair this? Può riparare questo?
pwo reepa-rahray kwaysto

Can you do it quickly? Può farlo presto?
pwo fahrlo presto

When can you get it done by? Quando potrà finirlo?
kwando potra fee-neerlo

I need some adhesive tape/a safety pin Ho bisogno di nastro adesivo/di una spilla di sicurezza
o beezohn-yo dee nastro aday-zeevo/dee oona speel-la dee seekoo-rayts-sa

The stitching has come undone Si è scucito
see e skoo-cheeto

Can you reheel these shoes? Può rifare i tacchi a queste scarpe?
pwo ree-fahray ee tak-kee a kwastay skarpay

The screw has come loose La vite si è allentata
la veetay see e al-layn-tahta

The handle has come off È uscita la maniglia
e oo-sheeta la maneel-ya

button il bottone
boht-tohnay

glue la colla
kol-la

hammer il martello
martel-lo

nail il chiodo
kee-odo

pin lo spillo
speel-lo

screwdriver il cacciavite
kat-cha-veetay

string lo spago
spahgo

tape il nastro
nastro

temporary temporaneo
taympo-rahnay-o

See also DRIVING ABROAD, ROAD SIGNS, WEATHER.
On the motorways (*autostrade*) you will have to stop periodically
to pay a toll (*pedaggio*). The outer (left) lane on the *autostrade* is
very definitely for overtaking.

**Is there a route that avoids the
traffic?** C'è un'altra strada per evitare il
traffico?
*che oonal-tra strahda payr ayvee-tahray eel
traf-feeko*

Is the traffic heavy on the motorway?
C'è molto traffico sull'autostrada?
che mohltoh traf-feeko sool-lowto-strahda

What is causing this hold-up? Perché
c'è questo ingorgo?
payrkay che kwaysto een-gorgo

When will the road be clear? Quando
sarà libera la strada?
kwando sara lee-bayra la strahda

Is there a detour? C'è una deviazione?
che oona dayvee-ats-yohnay

Is the road to ... snowed up? La strada
per ... è bloccata dalla neve?
la strahda payr ... e blok-kahta dal-la nayvay

Is the pass/tunnel open? È aperto il
passo/È aperta la galleria?
*e a-payrto eel pas-so/e a-payrta la gal-lay-
ree-a*

Do I need chains/studded tyres? C'è
bisogno di catene/gomme chiodate?
*che beezohn-yo dee ka-taynay/gohm-may
kee-o-dahtay*

accident
un incidente
eenchee-dentay
black ice
strada ghiacciata
strahda gee-atchah-ta
fog
la nebbia
nayb-ya
road conditions
le condizioni
stradali
*kondeets-yohnee
stra-dahlee*
road works
i lavori stradali
la-voree stra-dahlee
tailback
la coda
kohda
traffic jam
un ingorgo del
traffico
*een-gorgo dayl
traf-feeko*
**weather
conditions**
le condizioni
meteorologiche
*kondeets-yohnee
maytay-ohroh-lod-
jeekay*

See also DRIVING ABROAD, NOTICES

Accendere i fari
Switch on
  headlights

Altre direzioni
Other destinations

**Attenzione! dare la
  precedenza
  a destra**
Warning! Give way
  to traffic from
  right

Autostrada
Motorway

Banchina cedevole
Soft verge

Centro città
Town centre

Curve per 200m
Bends for 200m

Dare la precedenza
Give way

**Dare la precedenza
  a destra**
Give way to traffic
  coming from
  the right

Deviazione
Diversion

**Divieto di
  parcheggio**
No parking

**Divieto di transito
  ai pedoni**
Pedestrians
  prohibited

Dogana
Customs

**Fine divieto
  di parcheggio**
End of parking
  restrictions

**Fondo stradale
  dissestato**
Uneven road
  surface

Lavori in corso
Road works

Limite di velocità
Speed limit

Mantenere la destra
Keep right

Passaggio a livello
Level crossing

Pedaggio
Toll

Piazzola di sosta
Lay-by

**Possibilità di
  ghiaccio, superficie
  sdrucciolevole**
Icy road surface,
  Slippery road

Rallentare
Slow down

Senso unico
One way

**Strada con diritto
  di precedenza**
Priority road,
  You have
  priority

Strada panoramica
Scenic route

Strada sbarrata
Road closed

Strada senza uscita
No through road

Tutte le direzioni
Through traffic

Uscita d'emergenza
Emergency exit

Veicoli pesanti
Heavy goods
  vehicles

Vietato l'ingresso
No entry

Zona pedonale
Pedestrian precinct

See also COMPLAINTS, HOTEL DESK, TELEPHONE.

Come in! Avanti!
a-vantee

We'd like breakfast/a bottle of wine in our room
Vorremmo la colazione/una bottiglia di vino nella nostra
camera, per favore
*vor-**raym**-mo la kolats-**yoh**nay/oona bot-**teel**-ya dee veeno nayl-
la nostra **ka**-mayra payr fa-**vohray***

Put it on my bill Lo metta sul mio conto
lo mayt-ta sool mee-o kohntoh

I'd like an outside line, please Vorrei una linea con l'esterno,
per favore
*vor-**re**-ee oona **lee**nay-a kohn lay-**stayr**no payr fa-**vohray***

I have lost my key Ho perso la mia chiave
*o payrso la mee-a kee-**ahvay***

I have locked myself out of my room Sono rimasto chiuso
fuori della mia stanza
*sohnoh ree-**masto** kee-**oo**zo fworee dayl-la mee-a stantsa*

Where is the socket for my electric razor? Dov'è la presa
per il rasoio elettrico?
dohve la prayza payr eel razo-yo aylet-treeko

What's the voltage? Che voltaggio è?
kay voltad-jo e

I need a hairdryer/an iron Ho bisogno di un
asciugacapelli/un ferro da stiro
*o beezohn-yo dee oon ashoo-gaka-**payl**-lee/oon fer-ro da steero*

May I have an extra blanket/pillow? Posso avere un'altra
coperta/un altro guanciale?
*pos-so a-**vayray** oonal-tra ko-**payrta**/oon altro gwan-**chah**lay*

The TV/radio does not work La TV/radio non funziona
*la teevoo/rahd-yo nohn foonts-**yohna***

Can you send someone to collect my luggage? Potrebbe
mandare qualcuno a prendere i miei bagagli?
*po**treb**-bay man-**dah**ray kwal-**koo**no a **pren**-dayray ee
mee-**ay**-ee bagal-yee*

We are going aboard now Stiamo per imbarcarci adesso
stee-ahmo payr eembahr-kahrchee ades-so

The wind is getting up Si sta alzando il vento
see sta alt-sando eel vento

It's blowing hard from the north C'è vento forte dal nord
che vento fortay dal nord

It's flat calm C'è bonaccia
che bonat-cha

Ready about Pronti a virare
prohntee a vee-rahray

Hard to port/starboard Tutto a sinistra/a dritta
toot-to a see-neestra/a dreet-ta

We'll have to use the engine Dovremo usare il motore
dovraym-mo oo-zahray eel moh-tohray

When is the weather forecast? A che ora è il bollettino meteorologico?
a kay ohra e eel bol-layt-teeno maytay-ohroh-lo-jeekoh

We'll anchor here for the night Ancoriamo qui per stanotte
ankor-yahmo kwee payr stanot-tay

Please take my mooring rope Può prendere la mia cima d'ormeggio
pwo pren-dayray la mee-a cheema dormayd-jo

How does the toilet work? Come funziona il gabinetto?
kohmay foonts-yohna eel gabee-nayt-to

I'm feeling seasick Ho il mal di mare
o eel mal dee mahray

anchor	un'ancora *ankoh-ra*
boom	la boma *bohma*
bow	la prua *proo-a*
dinghy	il canotto *kanot-to*
halyard	la drizza *dreets-sa*
harbour	il porto *porto*
jib	il fiocco *fee-ok-ko*
mast	un albero *albay-ro*
propeller	un'elica *e-leeka*
rudder	il timone *tee-mohnay*
sail	la vela *vayla*
sheet	la scotta *skot-ta*
stern	la poppa *pohp-pa*

We've booked an apartment in the name of ... Abbiamo prenotato un appartamento a nome di ...
ab-yahmo prayno-tahto oon ap-parta-maynto a nohmay dee ...

Which is the key for the front door? Qual'è la chiave della porta principale?
kwahle la kee-ahvay dayl-la porta preenchee-pahlay

Where is the electricity meter? Dov'è il contatore dell'elettricità?
dohve eel kohnta-tohray dayl-laylet-treechee-ta

How does the shower work? Come funziona la doccia?
kohmay foonts-yohna la dot-cha

Is there a cleaner? C'è un'addetta alle pulizie?
che oonad-dayt-ta allay pooleet-see-ay

Is the cost of electricity included in the rental? Nell'affitto è compresa la luce?
nel-laf-feet-to e kom-prayza la loochay

Is there any spare bedding? Ci sono altre lenzuola e coperte?
chee sohnoh altray laynt-swola ay ko-payrtay

The toilet does not work Il gabinetto non funziona
eel gabee-nayt-to nohn foonts-yohna

A fuse has blown È fuso un fusibile
e foozo oon foozee-beelay

Where can I contact you? Dove posso mettermi in contatto con lei?
dohvay pos-so mayt-tayrmee een kontat-to kohn le-ee

bathroom
il bagno
ban-yo

bedroom
la camera da letto
ka-mayra da let-to

cooker
la cucina
koo-cheena

fridge
il frigorifero
freego-ree-fayro

gas
il gas
gas

kitchen
la cucina
koo-cheena

light
la luce
loochay

living room
la sala
sahla

sheet
il lenzuolo
laynt-swolo

toilet
la toilette
twalet

water heater
lo scaldabagno
skalda-ban-yo

See also BUYING, PAYING.

Where is the main shopping area?
Dove sono i negozi principali?
dohvay sohnoh ee nay-gotsee preenchee-pahlee

Where are the big stores? Dove sono i
grandi magazzini?
dohvay sohnoh ee grandee magadz-zeenee

What time do the shops close? A che
ora chiudono i negozi?
a kay ohra kee-oo-dohnoh ee nay-gotsee

How much does that cost? Quanto costa
quello?
kwanto kohsta kwayl-lo

How much is it per kilo/per metre?
Quanto costa al chilo/al metro?
kwanto kohsta al keelo/al metro

Can I try it on? Posso provarlo?
pos-so pro-vahrlo

Where is the food department? Dov'è il
reparto alimentari?
dohve eel ray-parto alee-mayn-tahree

I'm looking for a gift for my wife Sto
cercando un regalo per mia moglie
sto chayr-kando oon ray-gahlo payr mee-a mol-yay

I'm just looking Sto guardando solamente
sto gwar-dando sola-mayntay

**Have you anything suitable for a
small boy?** Avete qualcosa di adatto per
un bambino piccolo?
a-vaytay kwal-koza dee a-dat-to payr oon bam-beeno peek-kolo

Can I have a carrier bag please? Potrei
avere una busta di plastica?
potree-ee a-vayray oona boosta dee pla-steeka

cash desk
la cassa
kas-sa

changing room
lo spogliatoio
spol-yato-yo

closed
chiuso
kee-oozo

exit
un'uscita
o-sheeta

market
il mercato
mayr-kahto

open
aperto
a-payrto

paper bag
la busta
boosta

shopping bag
la borsa per la
spesa
borsa payr la spayza

stall
la bancarella
banka-rel-la

window
la vetrina
vay-treena

See also MAPS AND GUIDES, TRIPS AND EXCURSIONS.
Museum opening hours may be erratic and some sections can
rarely be visited at all. Churches open in the early morning, but usually close for three or four hours at noon.

What is there to see here? Che cosa c'è
da vedere qui?
kay koza che da vay-dayray kwee

**Excuse me, how do I get to the
cathedral?** Scusi, come faccio per andare
al duomo?
*skoozee kohmay fat-cho payr an-dahray al
dwomo*

**Where is the museum/the main
square?** Dov'è il museo/la piazza
principale?
*dohve eel mooze-o/la pee-ats-sa
preenchee-pahlay*

What time does the museum open? A
che ora apre il museo?
a kay ohra apray eel mooze-o

Is the castle open to the public? Il
castello è aperto al pubblico?
eel kastel-lo e a-payrto al poob-bleeko

Can we take photographs in here?
Possiamo fare delle fotografie qui dentro?
*pos-yahmo fahray dayl-lay foto-grafee-ay
kwee dayntro*

How much does it cost to get in?
Quanto costa il biglietto di entrata?
*kwanto kohsta eel beel-yayt-to dee ayn-
trahta*

Where can I buy some film/postcards?
Dove posso comprare un rullino/ delle
cartoline?
*dohvay pos-so kom-prahray oon rool-leeno/
dayl-lay karto-leenay*

guide book	la guida *gweeda*
map	la carta *kahrta*
park	il parco *pahrko*
souvenirs	i souvenirs *soovneer*
street plan	la piantina *pee-an-teena*
trip	la gita *jeeta*
view	la vista *veesta*

Tobacconists (*tabaccherie*) have a sign which is usually a black *T* on a white background. Look out for the "No Smoking" sign "VIETATO FUMARE".

Do you mind if I smoke? Le dispiace se fumo?
lay deespee-achay say foomo

May I have an ashtray? Posso avere un portacenere?
pos-so a-vayray oon porta-chay-nayray

Is this a no-smoking compartment/ area? Questo/Questa è uno scompartimento/una zona per non fumatori?
kwaysto/kwaysta e oono skompar-tee-maynto/oona zona payr nohn fooma-tohree

A packet of ... please Un pacchetto di ... per favore
oon pak-kayt-to dee ... payr fa-vohray

Have you got any American/English cigarettes? Avete delle sigarette americane/inglesi?
a-vaytay dell-lay seega-ret-tay amay-ree-kahnay/een-glayzee

I'd like some pipe tobacco Vorrei del tabacco per la pipa
vor-re-ee dayl tabak-ko payr la peepa

Do you have any matches/pipe cleaners? Avete dei fiammiferi/degli scovolini?
a-vaytay day-ee fee-am-mee-fayree/dayl-lyee skovo-leenee

Have you a gas refill for my lighter? Avete una bomboletta di gas per il mio accendino?
a-vaytay oona bombo-layt-ta dee gas payr eel mee-o at-chayn-deeno

Have you got a light? Ha da accendere?
a da at-chen-dayray

box of matches la scatola di fiammiferi
skah-tola dee fee-am-mee-fayree

brand la marca
mahrka

cigar il sigaro
see-garo

cigarette papers le cartine per sigarette
kahr-teenay payr seega-rayt-tay

filter il filtro
feeltro

filter-tipped con filtro
kohn feeltro

no smoking vietato fumare
vee-e-tahto foo-mahray

pipe la pipa
peepa

See also BEACH, ENTERTAINMENT, SAILING, WATERSPORTS, WINTER SPORTS.

Which sports activities are available here? Quali sport si possono fare qui?
kwahlee sport see pos-sono fahray kwee

Is it possible to go fishing/riding? Si può andare a pescare/a cavallo?
see pwo an-dahray a pay-skahray/a kaval-lo

Where can we play tennis/golf? Dove possiamo giocare a tennis/a golf?
dohvay pos-yahmo jo-kahray a tennis/a golf

Are there any interesting walks nearby? Ci sono delle belle passeggiate da fare qui vicino?
chee sohnoh dayl-lay bel-lay pas-sayd-jahtay da fahray kwee vee-cheeno

Can we rent the equipment? Possiamo noleggiare le attrezzature?
pos-yahmo nolayd-jahray lay at-trayts-sa-tooray

How much does it cost per hour? Quanto costa all'ora?
kwanto kohsta al-lohra

Do we need to be members? Bisogna essere soci?
beezohn-ya es-sayray sochee

Where do we buy our tickets? Dove si comprano i biglietti?
dohvay see kohm-prano ee beel-yayt-tee

Can we take lessons? Possiamo prendere delle lezioni?
pos-yahmo pren-dayray dayl-lay layts-yohnee

ball	
la palla	
pal-la	
climbing	
l'alpinismo	
alpee-neezmo	
cycling	
il ciclismo	
chee-kleezmo	
gym shoes	
le scarpe da ginnastica	
skahrpay da jeen-nas-teeka	
gymnasium	
la palestra	
pa-lestra	
hill-walking	
l'escursionismo	
ayskoors-yo-neezmo	
pony-trekking	
l'escursione a cavallo	
ayskoors-yohnay a kaval-lo	
racket	
la racchetta	
rak-kayt-ta	
shorts	
i calzoncini	
kaltson-cheenee	
squash	
lo squash	
squash	
swimming	
il nuoto	
nwoto	

adhesive tape
il nastro adesivo
nastro aday-zeevo

biro
la biro
beero

birthday card
il biglietto per compleanno
beel-yayt-to payr komplay-an-no

book
il libro
leebro

coloured pencils
i pastelli
pastel-lee

crayons
i pastelli a cera
pastel-lee a chayra

drawing book
un album di disegno
aloom dee deezayn-yo

envelopes
le buste
boostay

felt-tip pen
il pennarello
payn-narel-lo

file
il raccoglitore
rak-kohl-yee-tohray

glue
la colla
kol-la

ink
l'inchiostro
eenk-yostro

ink cartridge
la cartuccia
kartoot-cha

luggage tag
un'etichetta
aytee-kayt-ta

magazine
la rivista
ree-veesta

newspaper
il giornale
jor-nahlay

note pad
il libretto per appunti
leebrayt-to payr ap-poontee

painting book
il quaderno da colorare
kwa-dayrno da kolo-rahray

paints
i colori
koh-lohree

paper
la carta
kahrta

paperback
il tascabile
taskah-beelay

paperclip
il clip
kleep

pen
la penna
payn-na

pencil
la matita
ma-teeta

pencil sharpener
il temperamatite
taympay-rama-teetay

postcard
la cartolina
kahrto-leena

refill (for biro)
il ricambio
reekamb-yo

rubber
la gomma
gohm-ma

stapler
la cucitrice
koochee-treechay

staples
la graffetta
graf-fayt-ta

writing paper
la carta da lettera
kahrta da let-tayra

As a rule, taxis should be picked up at a stand rather than hailed. Make sure you are taking an official taxi - pirate cab operators are likely to overcharge you. Tip: around 15%.

Can you order me a taxi please? Può chiamarmi un taxi, per favore?
pwo kee-a-mahrmee oon taxee payr fa-vohray

To the main station Alla stazione centrale
al-la stats-yohnay chayn-trahlay

Take me to this address Mi porti a quest'indirizzo
mee portee a kwaysteen-deereets-so

Is it far? È lontano?
e lon-tahno

How much will it cost? Quanto verrà a costare?
kwanto ver-ra a ko-stahray

I'm in a hurry Ho molta fretta
o mohlta frayt-ta

Can you wait here for a few minutes? Può aspettare qui per alcuni minuti?
pwo aspayt-tahray kwee payr al-koonee mee-nootee

Turn left/right here Adesso giri a sinistra/a destra
ades-so jeeree a see-neestra/a destra

Please stop here/at the corner Si fermi qui/all'angolo per favore
see fayrmee kwee/ al-lan-golo payr fa-vohray

How much is it? Quant'è?
kwante

It's more than on the meter È più caro di quello indicato sul tassametro
e pee-oo kahro dee kwayl-lo eendee-kahto sool tas-sa-maytro

Keep the change Tenga il resto
tenga eel resto

Make it 15,000 lire Faccia 15.000 lire
fat-cha kweendee-chee-meela leeray

Can you give me a receipt? Può farmi una ricevuta?
pwo fahrmee oona reechay-voota

For international or long-distance calls go to the post office, where the official will give you tokens or a booth number. Many bars have telephones where you can make local calls and also long-distance calls if there is a sign *interurbano*. You will need *gettoni* (tokens), available at post offices, and it is wise to keep a supply of them. The ringing tone consists of long low bursts separated by short gaps, while the engaged tone has shorter bursts. Telephone numbers are given singly, so that 4321 would be four,three, two, one. (For numbers see p.64).

I want to make a phone call Voglio fare una telefonata
vol-yo fahray oona taylay-fo-nahta

Can I have a line? Posso avere la linea?
pos-so a-vayray la leenay-a

The number is 45 56 78, extension 89 Il numero è 45 56 78, interno 89
eel noo-mayre e kwat-tro cheenkway, cheenkway se-ee, set-tay ot-to, een-tayrno ot-to novay

I want to reverse the charges Voglio addebitare la spesa al ricevente
vol-yo ad-daybee-tahray la spayza al reechay-ventay

Have you got a telephone? C'è un telefono?
che oon tay-le-fono

How much is it to phone England? Quanto costa telefonare in Inghilterra?
kwanto kohsta taylay-fo-nahray een eengeel-ter-ra

I can't get through Non riesco a prendere la linea
nohn ree-esko a pren-dayray la leenay-a

The line's engaged La linea è occupata
la leenay-a e ok-koo-pahta

crossed line un interferenza
eentayr-fay-rentsa

dialling code il prefisso telefonico
prayfees-so taylay-fo-neeko

dialling tone il segnale di linea libera
sayn-yahlay dee leenay-a lee-bayra

directory un elenco telefonico
ay-lenko taylay-fo-neeko

operator il centralinista
chayntra-lee-neesta

phone box la cabina telefonica
ka-beena taylay-fo-neeka

receiver il ricevitore
reechay-vee-tohray

Hello, this is ... Pronto, sono ...
prohntoh sohnoh ...

Can I speak to Franco Rossi Posso parlare con Franco Rossi?
pos-so pahr-lahray kohn franco ros-see

I've been cut off Mi è stata tolta la communicazione
mee e stahta tolta la kom-moonee-kats-yohnay

It's a bad line Si sente male
see sayntay mahlay

You may hear:

Sto cercando di mettervi in comunicazione
sto chayr-kando dee mayt-tayrvee een komoo-neekats-yohnay
I'm trying to connect you

La sto mettendo in linea
la sto mayt-tayndo een leenay-a
I'm putting you through

Resti in linea
raystee een lee-nay-a
Hold the line

Mi dispiace, è occupato
mee deespee-achay e ok-koo-pahto
I'm sorry, it's engaged

Riprovi più tardi per favore
ree-prohvee pee-oo tardee payr fa-vohray
Please try again later

Chi chiama?
kee kee-ahma
Who's calling?

Scusi, ho sbagliato numero
skoozee o zbal-yahto noo-mayro
Sorry, wrong number

See also NUMBERS

What's the time?	**It's:**
Che ora è?/Che ore sono?	È/Sono
kay ohra eh/kay ohray sohnoh	*eh/sohnoh*

8.00	le otto
	lay ot-to
8.05	le otto e cinque
	lay ot-to ay cheen-kway
8.10	le otto e dieci
	lay ot-to ay dee-e-chee
8.15	le otto e un quarto
	lay ot-to ay oon kwarto
8.20	le otto e venti
	lay ot-to ay vayntee
8.25	le otto e venticinque
	lay ot-to ay vayntee-cheen-kway
8.30	le otto e mezza
	lay ot-to ay medz-za
8.35	le nove meno venticinque
	lay novay mayno vayntee-cheen-kway
8.40	le nove meno venti
	lay novay mayno vayntee
8.45	le nove meno un quarto
	lay novay mayno oon kwarto
8.50	le nove meno dieci
	lay novay mayno dee-e-chee
8.55	le nove meno cinque
	lay novay mayno cheen-kway
12.00	mezzogiorno
	medz-zo-jorno
	mezzanotte
	medz-za-not-tay

You may hear the 24-hour clock:

9.00pm	**21.00**	le ore ventuno
		lay ohray ven-toono
4.45pm	**16.45**	le diciassette meno un quarto
		lay deecha-set-tay mayno oon quarto
		kwarto

What time do you open/close? A che ora apre/chiude?
a kay ohra apray/kee-ooday

Do we have time to visit the town? Abbiamo tempo per
visitare la città?
ab-yahmo tempo payr veezee-tahray la cheet-ta

How long will it take to get there? Quanto ci vorrà per
arrivarci?
kwanto chee vor-ra payr ar-ree-vahrchee

We can be there in half an hour Possiamo arrivarci in
mezz'ora
pos-yahmo ar-ree-vahrchee een medz-zohra

We arrived early/late Siamo arrivati presto/tardi
see-ahmo ar-ree-vahtee presto/tardee

We should have been there two hours ago Dovremmo
essere là già da due ore
dovraym-mo es-sayray la ja da doo-ay ohray

We must be back at the hotel before 11 o'clock Dobbiamo
essere in albergo prima delle undici
*dob-yahmo es-sayray een al-bayrgo preema dayl-lay oon-
deechee*

When does the coach leave in the morning? A che ora
parte l'autobus alla mattina?
a kay ohra partay lowto-boos al-la mat-teena

The museum will be open in the morning/afternoon Il
museo sarà aperto di mattina/di pomeriggio
eel mooze-o sara a-payrto dee mat-teena/dee pomay-reed-jo

The table is booked for eight thirty this evening Il tavolo
è riservato per le otto e trenta di questa sera
*eel tah-volo e reezayr-vahto payr lay ot-to ay traynta dee kwaysta
sayra*

We'll be back very late Torneremo molto tardi
tornay-raymo mohltoh tahrdee

We'll be staying for a week/until 6th May Resteremo per
una settimana/fino al 6 maggio
raystay-raymo payr oona sayt-tee-mahna/feeno al se-ee mad-jo

See also TAXIS, TOILETS.

Your bill in cafés and restaurants will include a service charge - *Servizio Compreso* -, but any special service should be tipped for separately. In addition it is usual to leave the waiter any small coins from your change. Porters and chambermaids in hotels should be tipped, as should lavatory attendants - 100 lire - and theatre usherettes - 1,000 lire.

Sorry, I don't have any change Mi dispiace, non ho spiccioli
mee deespee-achay nohn o speet-cholee

Could you give me change of ...? Mi può dare ... in moneta?
mee pwo dahray ... een mo-nayta

Is it usual to tip ...? Si deve dare la mancia di ...?
see dayvay dahray la mancha dee ...

How much should I tip? Quanto devo lasciare di mancia?
kwanto dayvo la-shahray dee mancha

Keep the change Tenga pure il resto
tenga pooray eel resto

aftershave
il dopobarba
dopo-bahrba

baby wipes
i fazzolettini per
pulire i bambini
*fats-solayt-teenee
payr poo-leeray ee
bam-beenee*

cleansing cream
la crema
detergente
*krema daytayr-
jentay*

**contact lens
cleaner**
il liquido per lenti
a contatto
*leekweedo payr
lentee a kontat-to*

cotton wool
il cotone idrofilo
*koh-tohnay ee-
drofeelo*

deodorant
il deodorante
*day-oh-dohrantay
lyahta*

eye liner
la matita per occhi
*ma-teeta payr ok-
kee*

eye shadow
l'ombretto
ohmbrayt-to

eyebrow pencil
la matita per occhi
*ma-teeta payr ok-
kee*

face cloth
la spugnetta per il
viso
*spoon-yayt-ta payr
eel veezo*

hand cream
la crema per le
mani
*krema payr lay
mahnee*

lipstick
il rossetto
ros-sayt-to

mascara
la mascara
mascara

moisturizer
un idratante
eedra-tantay

nail file
la lima per unghie
*leema payr oong-
yay*

nail polish
lo smalto per
unghie
*zmalto payr oong-
yay*

**nail polish
remover**
l'acetone
achay-tohnay

perfume
il profumo
pro-foomo

razor
il rasoio
razo-yo

razor blades
le lamette
lamayt-tay

shampoo
lo shampoo
shampoo

shaving cream
la crema da barba
krema da barba

soap
la saponetta
sapo-nayt-ta

sponge
la spugna
spoon-ya

sun-tan cream
la crema
abbronzante
*krema ab-bront-
santay*

talc
il borotalco
boro-talko

tissues
i fazzoletti di carta
*fats-solayt-tee dee
kahrta*

toilet water
l'acqua di cologna
akwa dee kolon-ya

toothbrush
lo spazzolino da
denti
*spats-solee-no da
dentee*

toothpaste
il dentifricio
dayntee-freecho

Attendants who provide towels, soap etc should be tipped.

Where are the toilets, please? Dov'è la
toilette, per favore?
dohve la twalet payr fa-vohray

attendant
un addetto
ad-dayt-to

Where is the Gents'/the Ladies'? Dov'è
la toilette per Signori/per Signore?
dohve la twalet payr seen-yohree/seen-yohray

contraceptives
i contraccettivi
kontrat-chaytteevee

Do you have to pay? Bisogna pagare?
beezohn-ya pa-gahray

mirror
lo specchio
spek-yo

This toilet does not flush L'acqua non
esce da questo water
lakwa nohn e-shay da kwaysto vatayr

sanitary towels
gli assorbenti
as-sor-bayntee

There is no toilet paper/soap Non c'è
carta igienica/sapone
nohn che kahrta ee-je-neeka/sa-pohnay

seat
il cerchio del water
chayrk-yo dayl vatayr

**Do I have to pay extra to use the
washbasin?** Bisogna pagare di più per
usare il lavandino?
beezohn-ya pa-gahray dee pee-oo payr oo-zahray eel lavan-deeno

tampons
i tamponi
tam-pohnee

Is there a toilet for the disabled? C'è
una toilette per handicappati?
che oona twalet payr andee-kap-pahtee

**vending
machine**
il distributore
automatico
destree-boo-tohray owto-ma-teeko

**Are there facilities for mothers with
babies?** Ci sono dei servizi per madri con
bambini?
chee sohnoh day-ee sayr-veetsee payr mahdree kohn bam-beenee

waste bin
il bidone della
spazzatura
bee-dohnay dayl-la spats-satoo-ra

The towels have run out Gli
asciugamani sono finiti
lyee ashoo-ga-mahnee sohnoh fee-neetee

The door will not close La porta non si
chiude
la porta nohn see kee-ooday

See also RAILWAY STATION, LUGGAGE.

Is this the train for ...? È questo il treno per ...?
e kwaysto eel treno payr ...

Is this seat free? È libero questo posto?
e lee-bayro kwaysto pohstoh

I have a seat reservation Ho un posto prenotato
o oon pohstoh prayno-tahto

Can you help me put my suitcase on the luggage rack? Può aiutarmi a mettere la valigia sulla rete portabagagli?
pwo a-yoo-tahrmee a mayt-tayray la valeeja sool-la raytay porta-bagal-yee

May I open the window? Posso aprire il finestrino?
pos-so a-preeray eel feenay-streeno

What time do we get to ...? A che ora arriviamo a ...?
a kay ohra ar-reev-yahmo a ...

Do we stop at ...? Ci fermiamo a ...?
chee fayrm-yahmo a ...

Where do I change for ...? Dove devo cambiare per ...?
dohvay dayvo kamb-yahray payr ...

My wife has my ticket Mia moglie ha il mio biglietto
mee-a mol-yay a eel mee-o beel-yayt-to

Is there a buffet car/restaurant car? C'è una carrozza con ristorante?
che oona kar-rots-sa kohn reesto-rantay

Please tell me when we get to ... Per favore mi dica quando arriviamo a ...
payr fa-vohray mee deeka kwando ar-reev-yahmo a ...

alarm
un allarme
al-lahrmay

compartment
il compartimento
kompahr-tee-maynto

corridor
il corridoio
kor-reedo-yo

couchette
la cuccetta
koot-chayt-ta

driver
il macchinista
mak-kee-neesta

express
un espresso
aysprays-so

guard
il capotreno
kapo-trayno

sleeping car
il vagone letto
va-gohnay let-to

stopping train
un accelerato
at-chaylay-rahto

ticket collector
il controllore
kontrohl-lohray

toilet
la toilette
twalet

What's the best way to get to ...? Qual'è il modo migliore per andare a ...?
kwahle eel modoh meel-yohray payr an-dahray a ...

How much is it to fly to ...? Quanto costa andare in aereo a ...?
kwanto kohsta an-dahray een a-e-ray-o a ...

Are there any special cheap fares? Ci sono delle tariffe speciali?
chee sohnoh dayl-lay tareef-fay spay-chahlee

What times are the trains/flights? A che ora ci sono i treni/i voli?
a kay ohra chee sohnoh ee trenee/ee vohlee

Can I buy the tickets here? Posso comprare qui i biglietti?
pos-so kom-prahray kwee ee beel-yayt-tee

Can I change my booking? Posso cambiare la mia prenotazione?
pos-so kamb-yahray la mee-a prayno-tats-yohnay

Can you book me on the London flight? Può prenotarmi un posto sul volo di Londra?
pwo prayno-tahrmee oon pohstoh sool vohlo dee lohndra

Can I get back to Manchester tonight? Posso ritornare a Manchester questa notte?
pos-so reetor-nahray a manchester kwaysta not-tay

Two second class returns to ..., please Due biglietti di andata e ritorno, seconda classe per ..., per favore
doo-ay beel-yayt-tee dee an-dahta ay ree-torno say-kohnda klas-say payr ... payr fa-vohray

Can you book me into a hotel? Può prenotarmi un posto in albergo?
pwo prayno-tahrmee oon pohstoh een al-bayrgo

Do you do bookings for shows? Fate delle prenotazioni per spettacoli?
fahtay dayl-lay prayno-tats-yohnee payr spayt-tah-kolee

A ticket for tonight's performance please Un biglietto per lo spettacolo di questa sera, per favore
oon beel-yayt-to payr loh spayt-tah-kolo dee kwaysta sayra payr fa-vohray

See also SIGHTSEEING.

Are there any sightseeing tours? Ci
sono delle gite turistiche?
chee sohnoh dayl-lay jeetay tooree-steekay

When is the bus tour of the town?
Quando inizia il giro della città in
autobus?
*kwando eeneets-ya eel jeero dayl-la
cheeta-ta een ow-toboos*

How long does the tour take? Quanto
dura la gita?
kwanto doora la jeeta

**Are there any boat trips on the
river/lake?** Ci sono delle gite in barca sul
fiume/sul lago?
*chee sohnoh dayl-lay jeetay een barka sool
fee-oomay/sool lahgo*

**Are there any guided tours of the
cathedral?** Ci sono delle visite guidate
del duomo?
*chee sohnoh dayl-lay vee-zeetay gwee-
dahtay dayl dwomo*

**Is there a reduction for senior
citizens/children/groups?** C'è una
riduzione per pensionati/bambini/i
gruppi?
*che oona reedoots-yohnay payr payns-yo-
nahtee/bam-beenee/ee groop-pee*

Is there a commentary in English? C'è
un commento in inglese?
che oon kom-maynto een een-glayzay

Where do we stop for lunch? Dove ci
fermiamo per la colazione?
*dohvay chee fayrm-yahmo payr la kolats-
yohnay*

coach trip	la gita in autobus
	jeeta een ow-toboos
excursion	un'escursione
	ayskoors-yohnay
fare	la tariffa
	tareef-fa
organized	organizzato
	orga-needz-zahto
party	il gruppo
	groop-po
ticket	il biglietto
	beel-yayt-to
tour	il giro
	jeero
visit	la visita
	vee-zeeta
zoo	lo zoo
	dzo-oh

bottle opener
un apribottiglie
apree-boht-teel-yay

broom
la scopa
skohpa

can opener
un apriscatole
apree-ska-tohlay

chair
la sedia
sed-ya

cloth
lo straccio
stratch-yo

clothespeg
la molletta
mol-layt-ta

coat hanger
un attaccapanno
at-tak-kapan-no

comb
il pettine
pet-teenay

contact lenses
le lenti a contatto
lentee a kontat-to

corkscrew
il cavatappi
kava-tap-pee

cup
latazza
tat-tsa

dish
il piatto
pee-atto

elastic band
un elastico
aylas-teeko

flask
il thermos
termos

fork
la forchetta
forkayt-ta

frying-pan
la padella
padel-la

glasses
gli occhiali
ok-yahlee

hairbrush
la spazzola per capelli
spats-sola payr ka-payl-lee

hairgrip
il fermacapelli
fayrma-kapayl-lee

handkerchief
il fazzoletto
fats-solayt-to

knife
il coltello
koltel-lo

needle and thread
ago e filo
ahgo ay feelo

penknife
il temperino
taympay-reeno

plug
la spina
speena

rope
il cavo
kahvoh

safety pin
la spilla di sicurezza
speel-la dee seekoo-rayts-sa

saucepan
la pentola
payn-tola

scissors
le forbici
forbee-chee

spoon
il cucchiaio
kook-yah-yo

torch
la pila
peela

umbrella
un'ombrello
ombrel-lo

vacuum cleaner
un aspirapolvere
aspee-rapohl-vayray

washing up liquid
il detersivo per i piatti
daytayr-seevo payr ee pee-attee

See also BEACH, WINTER SPORTS.

Is it possible to go water-skiing/wind-surfing? Si può fare lo sci d'acqua/windsurf?
see pwo fahray loh shee dakwa/windsurf

Can we rent a motor boat/rowing boat? Possiamo affittare una barca a motore/una barca a remi?
pos-yahmo af-feet-tahray oona barka a moh-tohray/oona barka a raymee

Can I rent a sailboard? Posso affittare una tavola per il surf?
pos-so af-feet-tahray oona tah-vola payr eel surf

Can one swim in the river? Si può nuotare nel fiume?
see pwo nwo-tahray nayl fee-oomay

Can we fish here? Possiamo pescare qui?
pos-yahmo pay-skahray kwee

Is there a paddling pool for the children? C'è una piscina per bambini?
che oona pee-sheena payr bam-beenee

Do you give lessons? Dà lezioni?
da layts-yohnee

Where is the municipal swimming pool? Dov'è la piscina pubblica?
dohve la pee-sheena poob-bleeka

Is the pool heated? È riscaldata la piscina?
e reeskal-dahta la pee-sheena

Is it an outdoor pool? È una piscina all'aperto?
e oona pee-sheena al-lapayr-to

canoe
la canoa
kano-a

flippers
le pinne
peen-nay

goggles
gli occhiali
ok-yahlee

life jacket
il salvagente
salva-jentay

oar
il remo
remo

scuba-diving
l'attività subacquee
at-teevee-ta soo-bakway-ay

snorkel
il boccaglio
bok-kal-lyo

swimsuit
il costume da bagno
ko-stoomay da ban-yo

wetsuit
la muta
moota

It's a lovely day È una bella giornata
e oona bel-la jor-nahta

It's sunny C'è il sole
che eel sohlay

What dreadful weather! Che tempo
brutto!
kay tempo broot-to

It is raining/snowing Piove/nevica
pee-ovay/nay-veeka

It's windy C'è vento
che vento

There's a nice breeze blowing C'è un
bel venticello
che oon bel vayntee-chayl-lo

Will it be cold tonight? Farà freddo
stasera?
fara fred-do sta-sayra

Is it going to rain/to snow?
Pioverà/nevicherà?
pee-ovay-ra/nayvee-kayra

Will there be a frost? Ci sarà la brina?
chee sara la breena

Will there be a thunderstorm? Ci sarà un
temporale?
chee sara oon taympo-rahlay

Is it going to be fine? Sarà una bella
giornata?
sara oona bel-la jor-nahta

Is the weather going to change? Il
tempo cambierà?
eel tempo kamb-yayra

What is the temperature? Quanti gradi
ci sono?
kwantee gradee chee sohnoh

calm	calmo *kalmo*
clouds	le nuvole *noo-volay*
cool	fresco *fraysko*
fog	la nebbia *nayb-ya*
foggy	nebbioso *nayb-yohzo*
hot	molto caldo *mohltoh kaldo*
mild	mite *meetay*
mist	la foschia *foskee-a*
misty	nebbioso *nayb-yohzo*
warm	caldo *kaldo*
wet	piove *pee-ovay*

We'd like an aperitif Vorremmo un aperitivo
vor-raym-mo oon apay-ree-teevo

May I have the wine list please? Posso avere la lista dei vini?
pos-so a-vayray la leesta day-ee veenee

Can you recommend a good red/white/rosé wine? Ci può consigliare un buon vino rosso/bianco/rosato?
chee pwo konseel-yahray oon bwon veeno ros-so/bee-anko/ro-zahto

A bottle/carafe of house wine Una bottiglia/una caraffa di vino della casa
oona bot-teel-ya/oona karaf-fa dee veeno dayl-la kasa

A half bottle of ... Mezza bottiglia di ...
medz-za bot-teel-ya dee ...

Would you bring another glass please? Può portare un altro bicchiere per favore?
pwo por-tahray oon altro beek-ye-ray payr fa-vohray

This wine is not chilled Questo vino non è stato messo al fresco
kwaysto veeno nohn e stahto mays-so al fraysko

What liqueurs do you have? Quali liquori avete?
kwahlee lee-kwohree a-vaytay

I'll have a brandy/scotch/gin and tonic Prendo un brandy/un whisky/un gin con acqua tonica
prendo oon brandy/oon wheeskee/oon jeen kohn ak-kwa to-neeka

A Campari and soda Un Campari con seltz
oon campari kohn selts

champagne	lo champagne
	shampagne
dry	secco
	sayk-ko
medium	medio
	med-yo
port	il porto
	porto
sherry	lo sherry
	sherry
sparkling	frizzante
	freets-santay
sweet	dolce
	dohlchay
vermouth	il vermut
	vayrmoot
vodka	la vodka
	vodka

See also EATING OUT, WINES AND SPIRITS

Asti District producing red, white and sparkling white wine
Barbaresco Dry, full-bodied red wine (*Piedmont*)
Barbera Dry red wine (*Piedmont*)
Bardolino Light, dry red wine (*Veneto*)
Barolo Good, full-bodied red wine (*Piedmont*)
Chianti Dry red and white wines (*Tuscany*)
Chiaretto Dry rosé wine
Cinqueterre Good sweet and dry white wines (*Liguria*)
Frascati Dry to sweet white wine (*near Rome*)
Lacrima Christi Full-bodied red/white wine (*Campania*)
Lambrusco Slightly sparkling red wine
Malvasia Dessert wine
Marsala Dark dessert wine (*Sicily*)
Merlot Good, dry red wine
Montepulciano Dry or sweet red wine (*Tuscany*)
Moscato Dessert wine
Nebbiolo Light red wine, sweet or dry
Orvieto Sweet or semi-sweet white wine
Pinot Bianco Dry white wine
Sangiovese Good red wine
Savuto Dry red wine (*Calabria*)
Soave Dry white wine (*Verona*)
Valpolicella Light red wine
Verdicchio Dry white wine (*Marche*)
Verduzzo Dry white wine
Vernaccia Dry or sweet white wine

Vino bianco/rosso/rosato White/red/rosé wine
Vino dolce/abboccato/secco Sweet/semi-sweet/dry wine
Vino frizzante/spumante Semi-sparkling/sparkling wine
Vino locale Local wine
Vino da pasto/della casa Table/house wine

Can we hire skis here? Possiamo
noleggiare degli sci qui?
*pos-**yahmo** nolayd-**jahray** dayl-yee shee
kwee*

Could you adjust my bindings? Può
regolare i miei attacchi?
*pwo raygo-**lahray** ee mee-**e-ee** at-**tak**-kee*

A 3-day ticket please Un biglietto valido
per 3 giorni, per favore
*oon beel-**yayt**-to va-**leedo** payr tray jornee
payr fa-**vohray***

What are the snow conditions? Com'è
la neve?
kohme la nayvay

The snow is very icy/heavy La neve è
molto ghiacciata/pesante
*la nayvay e mohltoh gee-at-**chahta**/pay-
zantay*

**Is there a restaurant at the top
station?** C'è un ristorante alla stazione
d'arrivo?
*che oon reesto-**rantay** al-la stats-**yohnay**
dar-**reevo***

Which are the easiest runs? Quali sono
le piste più facili?
*kwahlee sohnoh lay peestay pee-oo fa-
cheelee*

We'll take the gondola Prendiamo la
seggiovia
*prend-**yahmo** la sayd-jovee-a*

When is the last ascent? Quand'è
l'ultima salita?
*kwan-**de** lool-teema sa-**leeta***

Is there danger of avalanches? C'è
pericolo di valanghe?
*che payre-**kolo** dee va-langay*

cablecar
la funivia
foonee-vee-a

chairlift
la seggiovia
sayd-jovee-a

goggles
gli occhiali da sci
*ok-**yahlee** da shee*

instructor
l'istruttore di sci
*eestroot-**tohray** dee
shee*

lift pass
la tessera per gli
impianti di risalita
*tes-sayra payr lyee
eempee-**ahn**-tee
dee reesa-**leeta***

rink
la pista di
pattinaggio
*peesta dee pat-
teenahd-jo*

skates
i pattini
pat-teenee

ski boots
gli scarponi da sci
*skar-**pohnee** da
shee*

ski pole
la racchetta da sci
*rak-**kayt**-ta da shee*

ski suit
il completo da sci
*kom-**pleto** da shee*

The following is a list of all the key words used in this book, with a cross reference to the topic(s) under which they appear. If you don't find the word you are looking for in the wordlist on any given page — look through the phrases.

bandage → ACCIDENTS –
  INJURIES, CHEMIST'S
bank → MONEY .
baptism → CELEBRATIONS
bar → ENTERTAINMENT, HOTEL
  DESK
bathroom → ACCOMMODATION
battery → CAR PARTS
beach → BEACH
beautiful → DESCRIBING THINGS
bed → DOCTOR
bedding → SELF-CATERING
bedroom → SELF-CATERING
beef → FOOD – GENERAL
beer → DRINKS
beetroot → FOOD – FRUIT AND
  VEG
begin, to → NIGHTLIFE
beige → COLOURS AND SHAPES
belt → CLOTHES
bend → DRIVING ABROAD
best wishes → CELEBRATIONS
big → CLOTHES, COLOURS AND
  SHAPES
bigger → BUYING
bill → EATING OUT, ORDERING,
  PAYING, ROOM SERVICE
biro → STATIONERY
birthday → CELEBRATIONS
birthday card → STATIONERY
bit, a b. → DENTIST
bite, to → ACCIDENTS – INJURIES
bitten → DOCTOR
bitter → DESCRIBING THINGS
black → COLOURS AND SHAPES,
  PHOTOGRAPHY
black coffee → DRINKS
black ice → ROAD CONDITIONS
blanket → ROOM SERVICE

bleeding → ACCIDENTS –
  INJURIES, DENTIST
blind → PERSONAL DETAILS
blood group → PERSONAL
  DETAILS
blood pressure → DOCTOR
blouse → CLOTHES
blow-dry → HAIRDRESSER'S
blue → COLOURS AND SHAPES
boat trip → TRIPS AND
  EXCURSIONS
body → BODY
bone → BODY
bonnet → CAR PARTS
book → STATIONERY
book of tickets → CITY TRAVEL
book, to → ENTERTAINMENT,
  TRAVEL AGENT
booking → HOTEL DESK, TRAVEL
  AGENT
booking office
  → ENTERTAINMENT
boot → CAR PARTS
bottle → CHILDREN, WINES AND
  SPIRITS
bottle opener → USEFUL ITEMS
bow → SAILING
box of matches → SMOKING
boy → CHILDREN
bra → CLOTHES
bracelet → GIFTS AND
  SOUVENIRS
brake fluid → CAR PARTS
brakes → CAR PARTS
brand → SMOKING
brandy → WINES AND SPIRITS
bread → FOOD – GENERAL
breakdown van → BREAKDOWNS

breakfast → ACCOMMODATION, ROOM SERVICE

breast → BODY

breathe, to → ACCIDENTS – INJURIES

breeze → WEATHER

bring, to → WINES AND SPIRITS

Britain → CONVERSATION – GENERAL, PERSONAL DETAILS

British → CUSTOMS AND PASSPORTS, PROBLEMS

broken → COMPLAINTS, REPAIRS

broken down → BREAKDOWNS

brooch → GIFTS AND SOUVENIRS

broom → USEFUL ITEMS

brown → COLOURS AND SHAPES

bucket → BEACH

buffet → RAILWAY STATION

buffet car → TRAIN TRAVEL

bulb → BREAKDOWNS

bureau de change → MONEY

bus → AIRPORT, CITY TRAVEL, COACH TRAVEL, TRIPS AND EXCURSIONS

bus depot → COACH TRAVEL

bus stop → CITY TRAVEL

bus tour → TRIPS AND EXCURSIONS

business → CUSTOMS AND PASSPORTS, PERSONAL DETAILS

business card → BUSINESS

butter → FOOD – GENERAL

buttocks → BODY

button → CLOTHES, REPAIRS

buy, to → GIFTS AND SOUVENIRS

cabaret → NIGHTLIFE

cabin → FERRIES

cablecar → WINTER SPORTS

café → EATING OUT

call, to → HOTEL DESK

calm → WEATHER

camera → PHOTOGRAPHY

camp, to → CAMPING AND CARAVANNING

camp-bed → CAMPING AND CARAVANNING

campsite → CAMPING AND CARAVANNING

can → PETROL STATION

can opener → USEFUL ITEMS

canoe → WATERSPORTS

captain → FERRIES

car → ACCIDENTS – CARS, AIRPORT, BREAKDOWNS, CAR HIRE

car documents → CAR HIRE

car number → POLICE

car park → DRIVING ABROAD

car wash → PETROL STATION

carafe → WINES AND SPIRITS

caravan → CAMPING AND CARAVANNING

carburettor → CAR PARTS

cardigan → CLOTHES

carrier bag → SHOPPING

carrots → FOOD – FRUIT AND VEG

cartridge → PHOTOGRAPHY

case → LUGGAGE

cash → MONEY, PAYING

cash advance → MONEY

cash desk → PAYING, SHOPPING

cashier → PAYING

casino → NIGHTLIFE

cassette → PHOTOGRAPHY

castle → SIGHTSEEING

catalogue → BUSINESS

catch, to → COACH TRAVEL

cathedral → CHURCH AND WORSHIP, SIGHTSEEING
Catholic → CHURCH AND WORSHIP
cauliflower → FOOD – FRUIT AND VEG
celery → FOOD – FRUIT AND VEG
chains → ROAD CONDITIONS
chair → USEFUL ITEMS
chairlift → WINTER SPORTS
champagne → WINES AND SPIRITS
change → BUYING, MONEY, TAXIS, WEATHER
change, to → AIRPORT, BEACH, CHILDREN, CITY TRAVEL, RAILWAY STATION
changing room → SHOPPING
Channel, the → FERRIES
chapel → CHURCH AND WORSHIP
charge → PAYING
chauffeur → CAR HIRE
cheap → EATING OUT, TRAVEL AGENT
cheaper → BUYING, PAYING
check in, to → AIRPORT, LUGGAGE
check, to → PETROL STATION
check-in desk → AIRPORT
cheek → BODY
cheers! → CELEBRATIONS
cheese → EATING OUT, FOOD – GENERAL
chemist's → ASKING QUESTIONS, CHEMIST'S
cheque → PAYING
cheque book → MONEY
cheque card → PAYING

cherries → FOOD – FRUIT AND VEG
chest → BODY
chicken → FOOD – GENERAL
child → CHILDREN
children → CHILDREN
chilled → WINES AND SPIRITS
chocolates → GIFTS AND SOUVENIRS
choke → CAR PARTS
christening → CELEBRATIONS
Christmas → CELEBRATIONS
church → CHURCH AND WORSHIP
churchyard → CHURCH AND WORSHIP
cigar → SMOKING
cigarette papers → SMOKING
cigarettes → SMOKING
cinema → ENTERTAINMENT
circular → COLOURS AND SHAPES
city → MAPS AND GUIDES
clean → DESCRIBING THINGS
clean, to → CLEANING, PETROL STATION
cleaner → SELF-CATERING
cleansing cream → TOILETRIES
clear → ROAD CONDITIONS
clerk → POST OFFICE
climbing → SPORTS
close → ACCIDENTS – CARS
close, to → SHOPPING, TIME PHRASES
closed → SHOPPING
cloth → USEFUL ITEMS
clothes → CLOTHES
clothespeg → USEFUL ITEMS
clouds → WEATHER
club → ENTERTAINMENT

clutch → CAR PARTS

coach trip → TRIPS AND EXCURSIONS

coastguard → EMERGENCIES

coat → CLOTHES

coat hanger → USEFUL ITEMS

coffee → FOOD – GENERAL

coke → DRINKS

cold → CHEMIST'S, DESCRIBING THINGS, WEATHER

collect, to → ROOM SERVICE

colour → CLOTHES, PHOTOGRAPHY

coloured pencils → STATIONERY

comb → USEFUL ITEMS

come off, to → REPAIRS

come out, to → CONVERSATION – MEETING

commentary → TRIPS AND EXCURSIONS

compartment → TRAIN TRAVEL

comprehensive → CAR HIRE

concert → ENTERTAINMENT

conditioner → HAIRDRESSER'S

conductor → CITY TRAVEL

confession → CHURCH AND WORSHIP

confirm, to → ACCOMMODATION

congratulations → CELEBRATIONS

connect, to → TELEPHONE

constipated → DOCTOR

consulate → EMERGENCIES

contact lens cleaner → TOILETRIES

contact lenses → USEFUL ITEMS

contact, to → SELF-CATERING

contraceptive → CHEMIST'S

controls → CAR HIRE

cooker → SELF-CATERING

cool → WEATHER

corkscrew → USEFUL ITEMS

corner → DIRECTIONS

corridor → TRAIN TRAVEL

cost, to → POST OFFICE, SHOPPING

cot → CHILDREN

cotton → CLOTHES

cotton wool → CHEMIST'S, TOILETRIES

couchette → TRAIN TRAVEL

cough → DOCTOR

counter → POST OFFICE

country → CUSTOMS AND PASSPORTS

courgettes → FOOD – FRUIT AND VEG

courrier → BUSINESS

course → ORDERING

cover charge → ORDERING

crayons → STATIONERY

cream → CHEMIST'S, FOOD – GENERAL

credit card → MONEY

crew → FERRIES

crimson → COLOURS AND SHAPES

crossed line → TELEPHONE

crossing → FERRIES

cube → COLOURS AND SHAPES

cucumber → FOOD – FRUIT AND VEG

cup → DRINKS

curly → HAIRDRESSER'S

currency → MONEY

current → BEACH

cut → DOCTOR, HAIRDRESSER'S

cut off → TELEPHONE

cut, to → ACCIDENTS – INJURIES
cycling → SPORTS
damage → ACCIDENTS – CARS
damage, to → LUGGAGE
dance, to → NIGHTLIFE
dark → COLOURS AND SHAPES
date → DATES AND CALENDAR
date of birth → PERSONAL
 DETAILS
daughter → PERSONAL DETAILS
day → WEATHER
dead → ACCIDENTS – INJURIES
deaf → PERSONAL DETAILS
deck → FERRIES
deck chair → BEACH
declare, to → CUSTOMS AND
 PASSPORTS
deep → BEACH
denim → CLOTHES
dentist → DENTIST
dentures → DENTIST
deodorant → TOILETRIES
department → BUYING
department store → BUYING
departure → RAILWAY STATION
deposit → PAYING
desk → HOTEL DESK
dessert → EATING OUT
details → BUSINESS
detour → ROAD CONDITIONS
develop, to → PHOTOGRAPHY
diabetic → DOCTOR
dialling code → TELEPHONE
dialling tone → TELEPHONE
diarrhoea → CHEMIST'S, DOCTOR
dictionary → MAPS AND GUIDES
diesel → PETROL STATION
difficult → DESCRIBING THINGS
dinghy → SAILING

dinner → HOTEL DESK
directory → TELEPHONE
dirty → COMPLAINTS,
 DESCRIBING THINGS
disabled → PERSONAL DETAILS,
 TOILETS
disco → NIGHTLIFE
discount → PAYING
dish → ORDERING, USEFUL
 ITEMS
disinfectant → CLEANING
dislocate, to → ACCIDENTS –
 INJURIES
disposable nappies → CHILDREN
distilled water → PETROL
 STATION
distributor → CAR PARTS
dizzy → DOCTOR
doctor → DOCTOR, EMERGENCIES
documents → ACCIDENTS –
 CARS, POLICE
dollars → MONEY
door → SELF-CATERING
double bed → ACCOMMODATION
double room
 → ACCOMMODATION
dozen → MEASUREMENTS
draught → DRINKS
drawing book → STATIONERY
dreadful → WEATHER
dress → CLOTHES
drink → EATING OUT
drinking chocolate → DRINKS
drinking water → CAMPING AND
 CARAVANNING, DRINKS
drive, to → CAR HIRE
driver → CITY TRAVEL, COACH
 TRAVEL, TRAIN TRAVEL
driving → CAR HIRE

driving licence → ACCIDENTS –
  CARS, DRIVING ABROAD
dry → WINES AND SPIRITS
dry cleaner's → CLEANING
dry, to → CLEANING
dummy → CHILDREN
duty-free → FERRIES
duty-free shop → AIRPORT
dynamo → CAR PARTS
ear → BODY
earache → DOCTOR
earrings → GIFTS AND
  SOUVENIRS
easy → DESCRIBING THINGS
eggs → FOOD – GENERAL
elastic band → USEFUL ITEMS
elbow → BODY
electric razor → ROOM SERVICE
electricity → SELF-CATERING
electrics → BREAKDOWNS
embassy → EMERGENCIES
emergency windscreen
  → BREAKDOWNS
engaged → TELEPHONE
engine → CAR PARTS, SAILING
England → POST OFFICE,
  TELEPHONE
English → PERSONAL DETAILS,
  PROBLEMS
enjoy → CELEBRATIONS
enough → MEASUREMENTS,
  MONEY, PAYING
entry visa → CUSTOMS AND
  PASSPORTS
envelopes → STATIONERY
equipment → SPORTS
escalator → CITY TRAVEL
evening → NIGHTLIFE

evening meal
  → ACCOMMODATION
excellent → DESCRIBING THINGS
excess luggage → LUGGAGE
exchange rate → MONEY
excursion → TRIPS AND
  EXCURSIONS
exhaust pipe → CAR PARTS
exhibition → BUSINESS
exit → SHOPPING
expect, to → BUSINESS
expensive → BUYING, PAYING
exposure meter
  → PHOTOGRAPHY
express → POST OFFICE, TRAIN
  TRAVEL
extension → TELEPHONE
extra → HOTEL DESK
eye → BODY
eye liner → TOILETRIES
eye shadow → TOILETRIES
eyebrow pencil → TOILETRIES
fabric → CLOTHES
face → BODY
face cloth → TOILETRIES
facilities → CHILDREN, TOILETS
factory → PERSONAL DETAILS
faint, to → DOCTOR
fall → ACCIDENTS – INJURIES
fan belt → CAR PARTS
far → DESCRIBING THINGS,
  DIRECTIONS
fare → CITY TRAVEL, TRAVEL
  AGENT, TRIPS AND EXCURSIONS
fast → ACCIDENTS – CARS,
  DESCRIBING THINGS
fat → COLOURS AND SHAPES
feed, to → CHILDREN
felt-tip pen → STATIONERY

festival → CELEBRATIONS
fetch, to → EMERGENCIES
file → STATIONERY
fill in, to → POST OFFICE
fill up, to → PETROL STATION
filling → DENTIST
film → NIGHTLIFE,
 PHOTOGRAPHY
film show → COACH TRAVEL
filter → SMOKING
filter-tipped → SMOKING
fine → GREETINGS, POLICE,
 WEATHER
finger → BODY
fire → EMERGENCIES
fire brigade → EMERGENCIES
first → EATING OUT
first class → RAILWAY STATION
fish → FOOD – GENERAL
fish, to → WATERSPORTS
fishing → SPORTS
flash → PHOTOGRAPHY
flash bulb → PHOTOGRAPHY
flash cube → PHOTOGRAPHY
flask → USEFUL ITEMS
flat tyre → BREAKDOWNS
flaw → COMPLAINTS
flight → AIRPORT
flight bag → LUGGAGE
flippers → WATERSPORTS
flour → FOOD – GENERAL
flowers → GIFTS AND SOUVENIRS
flush, to → TOILETS
fly, to → TRAVEL AGENT
fog → ROAD CONDITIONS,
 WEATHER
foggy → WEATHER
food → SHOPPING
food poisoning → DOCTOR

foot → BODY
forget, to → EMERGENCIES
forgotten → PROBLEMS
fork → USEFUL ITEMS
form → POST OFFICE
free → TRAIN TRAVEL
french beans → FOOD – FRUIT
 AND VEG
frequent → CITY TRAVEL
fridge → SELF-CATERING
fringe → HAIRDRESSER'S
frost → WEATHER
fruit juice → DRINKS
frying-pan → USEFUL ITEMS
full board → ACCOMMODATION
fun fair → ENTERTAINMENT
fur → CLOTHES
fuse → CAR PARTS, SELF-
 CATERING
garage → BREAKDOWNS, PETROL
 STATION
garlic → FOOD – FRUIT AND VEG
gas → SELF-CATERING
gas cylinder → CAMPING AND
 CARAVANNING
gas refill → SMOKING
gears → CAR PARTS
Gents' → TOILETS
Germany → POST OFFICE
get in, to → NIGHTLIFE,
 SIGHTSEEING
get off, to → CITY TRAVEL,
 COACH TRAVEL
get through, to → TELEPHONE
gift → SHOPPING
gift shop → GIFTS AND
 SOUVENIRS
gin → WINES AND SPIRITS
girl → CHILDREN

glass → DRINKS, WINES AND SPIRITS
glasses → USEFUL ITEMS
gloves → CLOTHES
glue → REPAIRS
goggles → WATERSPORTS
gold → COLOURS AND SHAPES
golf → SPORTS
good → ASKING QUESTIONS, DESCRIBING THINGS
good afternoon → GREETINGS
good evening → GREETINGS
good morning → GREETINGS
good night → GREETINGS
goodbye → GREETINGS
gown → HAIRDRESSER'S
gramme → BUYING, MEASUREMENTS
grapefruit → FOOD – FRUIT AND VEG
grapes → FOOD – FRUIT AND VEG
green → COLOURS AND SHAPES
green card → ACCIDENTS – CARS, POLICE
grey → COLOURS AND SHAPES
group → TRIPS AND EXCURSIONS
guard → RAILWAY STATION, TRAIN TRAVEL
guide book → MAPS AND GUIDES, SIGHTSEEING
guided tour → TRIPS AND EXCURSIONS
gums → DENTIST
guy rope → CAMPING AND CARAVANNING
gym shoes → SPORTS
gymnasium → SPORTS
hair → HAIRDRESSER'S
hair spray → HAIRDRESSER'S

hairbrush → USEFUL ITEMS
hairdryer → ROOM SERVICE
hairgrip → USEFUL ITEMS
half bottle → WINES AND SPIRITS
half fare → CITY TRAVEL
half-board → ACCOMMODATION
ham → FOOD – GENERAL
hammer → REPAIRS
hand → BODY
hand cream → TOILETRIES
hand luggage → LUGGAGE
hand-made → GIFTS AND SOUVENIRS
handbag → EMERGENCIES
handbrake → CAR PARTS
handkerchief → USEFUL ITEMS
handle → REPAIRS
harbour → SAILING
hard → DESCRIBING THINGS
hat → CLOTHES
hay fever → DOCTOR
hazard lights → BREAKDOWNS
head → BODY
headache → CHEMIST'S, DOCTOR
headlights → CAR PARTS
heart → BODY
heavy → DESCRIBING THINGS, LUGGAGE, ROAD CONDITIONS
hello → GREETINGS
help → EMERGENCIES
help! → EMERGENCIES
help, to → ASKING QUESTIONS, PROBLEMS
high chair → CHILDREN
high tide → BEACH
hill-walking → SPORTS
hire, to → AIRPORT, CAR HIRE
hold, to → TELEPHONE

hold-up → ROAD CONDITIONS

hole → COMPLAINTS

holiday → CELEBRATIONS, CONVERSATION - GENERAL

horrible → DESCRIBING THINGS

hose → CAR PARTS, PETROL STATION

hospital → ACCIDENTS - INJURIES

hot → DESCRIBING THINGS, WEATHER

hotel → AIRPORT, TRAVEL AGENT

hour → TIME PHRASES

house wine → WINES AND SPIRITS

hovercraft → FERRIES

hurry → TAXIS

hurt, to → ACCIDENTS - INJURIES, DENTIST

husband → PERSONAL DETAILS

ice → DRINKS

ice-cream → BEACH

icy → WINTER SPORTS

ignition → CAR PARTS

ill → DOCTOR

included → ORDERING, PAYING

indicator → CAR PARTS

inflamed → DOCTOR

information office → DIRECTIONS

injection → DENTIST, DOCTOR

injured → ACCIDENTS - INJURIES

ink → STATIONERY

ink cartridge → STATIONERY

insect bite → CHEMIST'S

insect repellant → CHEMIST'S

instructor → WINTER SPORTS

insurance certificate → ACCIDENTS - CARS, POLICE

insurance company → ACCIDENTS - CARS

insurance cover → CAR HIRE

interesting → DESCRIBING THINGS

international → POST OFFICE

Irish → PERSONAL DETAILS

iron → ROOM SERVICE

iron, to → CLEANING

Italian → CONVERSATION - MEETING

Italy → CONVERSATION - GENERAL

jack → BREAKDOWNS

jacket → CLOTHES

jam → FOOD - GENERAL

jam, to → PHOTOGRAPHY

jazz → ENTERTAINMENT

jeans → CLOTHES

joint → BODY

joint passport → CUSTOMS AND PASSPORTS

jump leads → BREAKDOWNS

keep, to → TAXIS

key → HOTEL DESK

kidney → BODY

kidneys → FOOD - GENERAL

kilo → BUYING, FOOD - GENERAL, MEASUREMENTS, SHOPPING

kilometre → ASKING QUESTIONS

kitchen → SELF-CATERING

knee → BODY

knife → USEFUL ITEMS

lace → CLOTHES

Ladies' → TOILETS

lake → TRIPS AND EXCURSIONS

lamb → FOOD – GENERAL
large → CAR HIRE
last, to → NIGHTLIFE
late → HOTEL DESK
later → TELEPHONE
launderette → CLEANING
laundry room → CLEANING
laundry service → CLEANING
lavatory → PETROL STATION
law → ACCIDENTS – CARS
lawyer → ACCIDENTS – CARS,
  POLICE
laxative → CHEMIST'S
layered → HAIRDRESSER'S
leak → BREAKDOWNS
leather → CLOTHES
leave, to → COACH TRAVEL,
  TIME PHRASES
leeks → FOOD – FRUIT AND VEG
left → DIRECTIONS
left luggage → LUGGAGE,
  RAILWAY STATION
leg → BODY
lemon → COLOURS AND SHAPES,
  FOOD – FRUIT AND VEG
lemon tea → DRINKS
lemonade → DRINKS
lens → PHOTOGRAPHY
lens cover → PHOTOGRAPHY
less → MEASUREMENTS
lessons → SPORTS
let off, to → COACH TRAVEL
letter → POST OFFICE
lettuce → FOOD – FRUIT AND
  VEG
life jacket → FERRIES,
  WATERSPORTS
lifeboat → FERRIES
lifeguard → BEACH

lift → ACCOMMODATION
light → CLOTHES, COLOURS AND
  SHAPES, DESCRIBING THINGS,
  SELF-CATERING, SMOKING
lighter → SMOKING
like, to → CONVERSATION –
  GENERAL
line → TELEPHONE
lipstick → TOILETRIES
liqueur → WINES AND SPIRITS
lire → MONEY
literature → BUSINESS
litre → FOOD – GENERAL,
  MEASUREMENTS, PETROL
  STATION
live, to → PERSONAL DETAILS
liver → BODY, FOOD – GENERAL
living room → SELF-CATERING
local → MAPS AND GUIDES,
  ORDERING
lock → COMPLAINTS
locked out → ROOM SERVICE
locker → LUGGAGE
long → COLOURS AND SHAPES,
  DESCRIBING THINGS, FERRIES,
  HAIRDRESSER'S
look for, to → SHOPPING
loose → REPAIRS
lost property office
  → EMERGENCIES
lounge → AIRPORT, HOTEL DESK
lovely → DESCRIBING THINGS,
  WEATHER
low tide → BEACH
luggage → LUGGAGE
luggage allowance → LUGGAGE
luggage hold → COACH TRAVEL
luggage rack → LUGGAGE
luggage tag → STATIONERY

luggage trolley → LUGGAGE
lunch → EATING OUT
lung → BODY
magazine → STATIONERY
main → SHOPPING
main course → EATING OUT
major road → DRIVING ABROAD
mallet → CAMPING AND CARAVANNING
manage, to → LUGGAGE
manager → HOTEL DESK
map → MAPS AND GUIDES
margarine → FOOD – GENERAL
market → SHOPPING
Martini → WINES AND SPIRITS
mascara → TOILETRIES
mass → CHURCH AND WORSHIP
mast → SAILING
matches → SMOKING
material → CLOTHES
mauve → COLOURS AND SHAPES
meal → ORDERING
measure, to → CLOTHES
mechanic → BREAKDOWNS
medicine → DOCTOR
medium → WINES AND SPIRITS
medium rare → ORDERING
melon → FOOD – FRUIT AND VEG
member → NIGHTLIFE
menu → EATING OUT, ORDERING
message → BUSINESS
meter → SELF-CATERING, TAXIS
metre → SHOPPING
mild → WEATHER
milk → DRINKS, FOOD – GENERAL
mince → FOOD – GENERAL
mind, to → SMOKING
mineral water → DRINKS

minister → CHURCH AND WORSHIP
minor road → DRIVING ABROAD
minute → TIME
mirror → TOILETS
missing → EMERGENCIES
mist → WEATHER
misty → WEATHER
moisturizer → TOILETRIES
money → MONEY
money order → POST OFFICE
more → GIFTS AND SOUVENIRS, MEASUREMENTS
morning → TIME PHRASES
mosque → CHURCH AND WORSHIP
mother → TOILETS
motor boat → WATERSPORTS
motorway → DRIVING ABROAD
mouth → BODY
move, to → ACCIDENTS – INJURIES
movie camera → PHOTOGRAPHY
municipal → WATERSPORTS
muscle → BODY
museum → SIGHTSEEING
mushrooms → FOOD – FRUIT AND VEG
mustard → FOOD – GENERAL
nail → REPAIRS
nail file → TOILETRIES
nail polish → TOILETRIES
nail polish remover → TOILETRIES
name → PERSONAL DETAILS
nappy → CHILDREN
national → CUSTOMS AND PASSPORTS

near → DESCRIBING THINGS, DIRECTIONS
nearest → DIRECTIONS
neck → BODY
necklace → GIFTS AND SOUVENIRS
need, to → DOCTOR
needle and thread → USEFUL ITEMS
negative → PHOTOGRAPHY
new → DESCRIBING THINGS
New Year → CELEBRATIONS
newspaper → STATIONERY
next → FERRIES, RAILWAY STATION
nice → WEATHER
night → HOTEL DESK
night club → NIGHTLIFE
nightdress → CLOTHES
no → CONVERSATION – MEETING
no smoking → SMOKING
noisy → COMPLAINTS
non-smoking → AIRPORT, RAILWAY STATION
nose → BODY
note → MONEY
note pad → STATIONERY
number → PERSONAL DETAILS
nylon → CLOTHES
oar → WATERSPORTS
oblong → COLOURS AND SHAPES
offence → ACCIDENTS – CARS
office → PERSONAL DETAILS
officer → POLICE
oil → FOOD – GENERAL, PETROL STATION
old → DESCRIBING THINGS
olives → FOOD – FRUIT AND VEG
one-way → DRIVING ABROAD

onions → FOOD – FRUIT AND VEG
open → SHOPPING
open, to → SIGHTSEEING, TIME PHRASES
operate, to → CAR HIRE
operation → DOCTOR
operator → TELEPHONE
orange → COLOURS AND SHAPES
oranges → FOOD – FRUIT AND VEG
orchestra → ENTERTAINMENT
order → ORDERING
organized → TRIPS AND EXCURSIONS
ornament → GIFTS AND SOUVENIRS
outside line → ROOM SERVICE
oval → COLOURS AND SHAPES
over → DIRECTIONS
over there → DIRECTIONS
overheat, to → BREAKDOWNS
packet → SMOKING
paddling pool → WATERSPORTS
pain → DOCTOR
painful → DOCTOR
painting book → STATIONERY
paints → STATIONERY
panties → CLOTHES
pants → CLOTHES
paper → STATIONERY
paper bag → SHOPPING
paperback → STATIONERY
paperclip → STATIONERY
parcel → POST OFFICE
park → SIGHTSEEING
park, to → DRIVING ABROAD
parking disk → DRIVING ABROAD

parking meter → DRIVING ABROAD
parking ticket → DRIVING ABROAD
parting → HAIRDRESSER'S
parts → BREAKDOWNS
party → TRIPS AND EXCURSIONS
pass → ROAD CONDITIONS
passport → EMERGENCIES, PERSONAL DETAILS
passport control → AIRPORT
pay, to → PAYING
payment → PAYING
peaches → FOOD − FRUIT AND VEG
pears → FOOD − FRUIT AND VEG
peas → FOOD − FRUIT AND VEG
pen → STATIONERY
pencil → STATIONERY
pencil sharpener → STATIONERY
penicillin → DOCTOR
penknife → USEFUL ITEMS
pepper → FOOD − FRUIT AND VEG, FOOD − GENERAL
per → CAMPING AND CARAVANNING
performance → NIGHTLIFE
perfume → TOILETRIES
perm → HAIRDRESSER'S
permed → HAIRDRESSER'S
petrol → BREAKDOWNS, PETROL STATION
petrol pump → PETROL STATION
petrol station → PETROL STATION
petrol tank → BREAKDOWNS
petticoat → CLOTHES
phone box → TELEPHONE
phone call → TELEPHONE

phone, to → TELEPHONE
photocopy, to → BUSINESS
photos → PHOTOGRAPHY
phrase book → MAPS AND GUIDES
picnic → HOTEL DESK
pill → DOCTOR
pin → REPAIRS
pineapple → FOOD − FRUIT AND VEG
pink → COLOURS AND SHAPES
pint → MEASUREMENTS
pipe → SMOKING
pipe cleaners → SMOKING
pipe tobacco → SMOKING
plane → AIRPORT
plate → USEFUL ITEMS
platform → RAILWAY STATION
play → ENTERTAINMENT
play, to → ENTERTAINMENT, SPORTS
playroom → CHILDREN
pleasant → DESCRIBING THINGS
plug → USEFUL ITEMS
plums → FOOD − FRUIT AND VEG
pointed → COLOURS AND SHAPES
points → CAR PARTS
poisoning → DOCTOR
police → ACCIDENTS − CARS, POLICE
police car → POLICE
police station → POLICE
policeman → POLICE
polyester → CLOTHES
pony-trekking → SPORTS
pork → FOOD − GENERAL
port → WINES AND SPIRITS
porter → HOTEL DESK, LUGGAGE
portion → MEASUREMENTS

possible → SPORTS
post office → POST OFFICE
postage → POST OFFICE
postcard → STATIONERY
pot → DRINKS
potatoes → FOOD – FRUIT AND VEG
pottery → GIFTS AND SOUVENIRS
pound → FOOD – GENERAL, MEASUREMENTS
pounds → MONEY
pram → CHILDREN
prefer, to → BUYING
pregnant → DOCTOR
prescription → CHEMIST'S
present → GIFTS AND SOUVENIRS
priest → CHURCH AND WORSHIP
prints → PHOTOGRAPHY
private → BEACH
propeller → SAILING
Protestant → CHURCH AND WORSHIP
public → SIGHTSEEING
public holiday → CELEBRATIONS
purple → COLOURS AND SHAPES
purse → MONEY
purser → FERRIES
push chair → CHILDREN
put through, to → TELEPHONE
put, to → ROOM SERVICE
pyjamas → CLOTHES
quarter → MEASUREMENTS
quickly → EMERGENCIES
quiet → BEACH
rabbi → CHURCH AND WORSHIP
racket → SPORTS
radiator → CAR PARTS
radio → CAR HIRE
radio-cassette → CAR HIRE

radishes → FOOD – FRUIT AND VEG
rain, to → WEATHER
raincoat → CLOTHES
rare → ORDERING
raspberries → FOOD – FRUIT AND VEG
rate → MONEY
razor → TOILETRIES
razor blades → TOILETRIES
ready → ASKING QUESTIONS
receipt → PAYING
receiver → TELEPHONE
reclining seat → FERRIES
recommend, to → ORDERING
red → COLOURS AND SHAPES, WINES AND SPIRITS
reduction → PAYING
reel → PHOTOGRAPHY
refill → STATIONERY
regional → GIFTS AND SOUVENIRS
registered → POST OFFICE
regulations → POLICE
reheel, to → REPAIRS
reimburse, to → MONEY
remove, to → CLEANING
rent, to → SPORTS
rental → SELF-CATERING
repair, to → REPAIRS
repeat, to → PROBLEMS
reply coupon → POST OFFICE
reservation → HOTEL DESK, RAILWAY STATION
reserve, to → AIRPORT, HOTEL DESK, RAILWAY STATION
restaurant → EATING OUT
restaurant car → TRAIN TRAVEL
return → RAILWAY STATION

return ticket → FERRIES
reversing lights → CAR PARTS
rice → FOOD – GENERAL
riding → SPORTS
right → DIRECTIONS
ring → GIFTS AND SOUVENIRS
rink → WINTER SPORTS
river → WATERSPORTS
road → DRIVING ABROAD
road conditions → ROAD
  CONDITIONS
road map → MAPS AND GUIDES
road sign → DIRECTIONS
road works → ROAD CONDITIONS
rob, to → POLICE
room → HOTEL DESK
room service → HOTEL DESK
rope → USEFUL ITEMS
rosé → WINES AND SPIRITS
rough → DESCRIBING THINGS,
  FERRIES
round → COLOURS AND SHAPES
route → ROAD CONDITIONS
rowing boat → WATERSPORTS
rubber → STATIONERY
rudder → SAILING
run out, to → BREAKDOWNS,
  PROBLEMS
safe → BEACH
safety pin → REPAIRS, USEFUL
  ITEMS
sail → SAILING
sailboard → WATERSPORTS
sailing → FERRIES
salt → FOOD – GENERAL
sample → BUSINESS
sandals → CLOTHES
sandwich → EATING OUT
sanitary towels → CHEMIST'S

saucepan → USEFUL ITEMS
scarf → CLOTHES
scissors → USEFUL ITEMS
Scotch → WINES AND SPIRITS
Scottish → PERSONAL DETAILS
screw → REPAIRS
screwdriver → REPAIRS
scuba-diving → WATERSPORTS
sea → BEACH, FERRIES
seasick → SAILING
season ticket → CITY TRAVEL
seat → COACH TRAVEL, RAILWAY
  STATION, TOILETS, TRAIN
  TRAVEL
seat belt → DRIVING ABROAD
seat reservation → TRAIN
  TRAVEL
second class → RAILWAY
  STATION, TRAVEL AGENT
secretary → BUSINESS
see, to → SIGHTSEEING
sell, to → BUYING
send, to → POST OFFICE
senior citizen → TRIPS AND
  EXCURSIONS
serious → ACCIDENTS – INJURIES
serve, to → ORDERING
served, to be → COMPLAINTS
service → CHURCH AND
  WORSHIP, ORDERING
set → HAIRDRESSER'S
shade → COLOURS AND SHAPES
shampoo → TOILETRIES
shandy → DRINKS
shattered → BREAKDOWNS
shaving cream → TOILETRIES
sheet → SELF-CATERING
sherry → WINES AND SPIRITS
shiny → COLOURS AND SHAPES

ship → FERRIES
shirt → CLOTHES
shock absorber → CAR PARTS
shoes → CLOTHES
shop → BUYING
shopping area → SHOPPING
shopping bag → SHOPPING
short → DESCRIBING THINGS,
  HAIRDRESSER'S
short cut → DRIVING ABROAD
shorts → CLOTHES, SPORTS
shoulder → BODY
show → NIGHTLIFE
show, to → DIRECTIONS, MAPS
  AND GUIDES
shower → SELF-CATERING
sick → DOCTOR, TRIPS AND
  EXCURSIONS
sightseeing → TRIPS AND
  EXCURSIONS
sign → DRIVING ABROAD
signature → PAYING
silk → CLOTHES
silver → COLOURS AND SHAPES
single → RAILWAY STATION
single bed → ACCOMMODATION
single room
  → ACCOMMODATION
sink → CLEANING
sit, to → CONVERSATION –
  MEETING
site → CAMPING AND
  CARAVANNING
skates → WINTER SPORTS
skating → WINTER SPORTS
ski boot → WINTER SPORTS
ski pole → WINTER SPORTS
skin → BODY
skirt → CLOTHES

skis → WINTER SPORTS
sleep, to → DOCTOR
sleeper → RAILWAY STATION
sleeping bag → CAMPING AND
  CARAVANNING
sleeping car → TRAIN TRAVEL
slice → MEASUREMENTS
slides → PHOTOGRAPHY
slip, to → ACCIDENTS – INJURIES
slow → DESCRIBING THINGS
small → COLOURS AND SHAPES
smaller → BUYING
smoke, to → SMOKING
smooth → DESCRIBING THINGS,
  FERRIES
snack bar → AIRPORT
snorkel → WATERSPORTS
snow → WINTER SPORTS
snow, to → WEATHER
snowed up → ROAD CONDITIONS
soap → TOILETRIES
socket → ROOM SERVICE
socks → CLOTHES
soft → DESCRIBING THINGS
soft drink → DRINKS
son → PERSONAL DETAILS
sore → CHEMIST'S, DENTIST,
  DOCTOR
sorry → CONVERSATION –
  GENERAL
soup → EATING OUT, FOOD –
  GENERAL
sour → DESCRIBING THINGS
souvenir → GIFTS AND
  SOUVENIRS
spade → BEACH
spanner → BREAKDOWNS
spare → SELF-CATERING
spark plugs → CAR PARTS

sparkling → WINES AND SPIRITS

speak, to → CONVERSATION – MEETING, TELEPHONE

special → TRAVEL AGENT

special rate → CHILDREN

speciality → ORDERING

speed limit → DRIVING ABROAD

spicy → DESCRIBING THINGS

spinach → FOOD – FRUIT AND VEG

spirits → CUSTOMS AND PASSPORTS

sponge → TOILETRIES

spoon → USEFUL ITEMS

sports → SPORTS

sprain → ACCIDENTS – INJURIES

square → COLOURS AND SHAPES

squash → SPORTS

stain → CLEANING

stall → SHOPPING

stamps → POST OFFICE

stapler → STATIONERY

staples → STATIONERY

starter → EATING OUT

station → TAXIS

stay → HOTEL DESK

stay, to → CUSTOMS AND PASSPORTS, DOCTOR

steak → FOOD – GENERAL

steering → CAR PARTS

steering wheel → CAR PARTS

sterling → MONEY

stern → SAILING

sticking plaster → CHEMIST'S

stitching → REPAIRS

stockings → CLOTHES

stolen → EMERGENCIES

stomach → BODY

stomach upset → DOCTOR

stop, to → TAXIS, TRAIN TRAVEL, TRIPS AND EXCURSIONS

stopping train → TRAIN TRAVEL

straight → HAIRDRESSER'S

straight on → DIRECTIONS

strawberries → FOOD – FRUIT AND VEG

streaks → HAIRDRESSER'S

street map → MAPS AND GUIDES

street plan → SIGHTSEEING

string → REPAIRS

strong → DESCRIBING THINGS

student → PERSONAL DETAILS

stung → ACCIDENTS – INJURIES

styling mousse → HAIRDRESSER'S

suede → CLOTHES

sugar → FOOD – GENERAL

suit (man's) → CLOTHES

suit (woman's) → CLOTHES

suitable → SHOPPING

suitcase → LUGGAGE

sun-tan cream → TOILETRIES

sunburn → ACCIDENTS – INJURIES

sunglasses → BEACH

sunny → WEATHER

sunshade → BEACH

sunstroke → ACCIDENTS – INJURIES

suntan oil → BEACH

supermarket → BUYING

swallow, to → DOCTOR

sweater → CLOTHES

sweet → DESCRIBING THINGS, WINES AND SPIRITS

swim, to → BEACH

swimming → SPORTS

swimming pool
 → WATERSPORTS
swimsuit → BEACH, CLOTHES
synagogue → CHURCH AND
 WORSHIP
t-shirt → CLOTHES
table → EATING OUT, ORDERING
table linen → GIFTS AND
 SOUVENIRS
tablet → DOCTOR
tailback → ROAD CONDITIONS
take out, to → DENTIST
take up, to → HOTEL DESK
take, to → CHEMIST'S,
 DIRECTIONS, SPORTS
talc → TOILETRIES
tampons → CHEMIST'S
tap → CLEANING
tape → REPAIRS
tax → PAYING
taxi → TAXIS
tea → DRINKS, FOOD – GENERAL
telegram → POST OFFICE
telephone → TELEPHONE
telex → BUSINESS
tell, to → TRAIN TRAVEL
temperature → DOCTOR,
 WEATHER
temporary → REPAIRS
tennis → SPORTS
tent → CAMPING AND
 CARAVANNING
tent peg → CAMPING AND
 CARAVANNING
tent pole → CAMPING AND
 CARAVANNING
terrace → EATING OUT
thank you → CONVERSATION –
 MEETING

that one → ORDERING
theatre → ENTERTAINMENT
thick → COLOURS AND SHAPES
thin → COLOURS AND SHAPES
things → CLEANING
third → MEASUREMENTS
this one → ORDERING
throat → BODY
through → DIRECTIONS
thumb → BODY
thunderstorm → WEATHER
ticket → CITY TRAVEL,
 ENTERTAINMENT, TRIPS AND
 EXCURSIONS
ticket collector → TRAIN TRAVEL
ticket office → RAILWAY
 STATION
tie → CLOTHES
tights → CLOTHES
till → PAYING
time → TIME, TIME PHRASES
timetable board → RAILWAY
 STATION
tin → FOOD – GENERAL
tinted → COLOURS AND SHAPES
tip, to → TIPPING
tissues → TOILETRIES
tobacco → CUSTOMS AND
 PASSPORTS
toe → BODY
toilet → TOILETS
toilet paper → TOILETS
toilet water → TOILETRIES
toll → DRIVING ABROAD
tomatoes → FOOD – FRUIT AND
 VEG
tomorrow → BUSINESS
tongue → BODY
tonight → NIGHTLIFE

too → CLOTHES
tooth → DENTIST
toothache → DENTIST
toothbrush → TOILETRIES
toothpaste → TOILETRIES
torch → USEFUL ITEMS
torn → REPAIRS
tour → TRIPS AND EXCURSIONS
tourist → DIRECTIONS
tourist office → MAPS AND
  GUIDES
tourist ticket → CITY TRAVEL
tow rope → BREAKDOWNS
tow, to → BREAKDOWNS
towel → BEACH, HAIRDRESSER'S
town → CITY TRAVEL
town centre → CITY TRAVEL
town plan → MAPS AND GUIDES
trade fair → BUSINESS
traffic → ROAD CONDITIONS
traffic jam → ROAD CONDITIONS
traffic lights → DRIVING
  ABROAD
traffic offence → POLICE
traffic warden → POLICE
trailer → CAMPING AND
  CARAVANNING
train → CITY TRAVEL, TRAIN
  TRAVEL
transfer, to → MONEY
transit, in t. → LUGGAGE
travel, to → GIFTS AND
  SOUVENIRS
traveller's cheques → MONEY
trim → HAIRDRESSER'S
trip → SIGHTSEEING
tripod → PHOTOGRAPHY
trouble → PROBLEMS
trousers → CLOTHES

trunk → LUGGAGE
trunks → CLOTHES
try on, to → CLOTHES
tunnel → ROAD CONDITIONS
turn off, to → COMPLAINTS
turn on, to → COMPLAINTS
turn, to → TAXIS
turning → DIRECTIONS
turquoise → COLOURS AND
  SHAPES
TV lounge → HOTEL DESK
twice → MEASUREMENTS
tyre → CAR PARTS
tyre pressure → PETROL
  STATION
umbrella → USEFUL ITEMS
unconscious → DOCTOR
under → DIRECTIONS
underground train → CITY
  TRAVEL
understand, to → ASKING
  QUESTIONS
unpleasant → DESCRIBING
  THINGS
upset → CHEMIST'S
urgently → DENTIST
use, to → TOILETS
vacancies → CAMPING AND
  CARAVANNING
vacuum cleaner → USEFUL
  ITEMS
veal → FOOD – GENERAL
vegetables → EATING OUT
vending machine → TOILETS
vermouth → WINES AND SPIRITS
vest → CLOTHES
view → SIGHTSEEING
vinegar → FOOD – GENERAL
visit → TRIPS AND EXCURSIONS